Cambridge problems in
physics and advice
on solutions

Second edition

£9.95

Cambridge problems in physics and advice on solutions

Second edition

Edited for the
University of Cambridge Local Examinations Syndicate by

P.P. Dendy, R. Tuffnell and C.H.B. Mee

The South East Essex   C R
College of Arts & Technology
Carnarvon Road   Southend on Sea   Essex   SS2 6LS
Tel: Southend (0702) 220400   Fax: Southend (0702) 432320

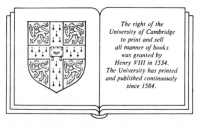

The right of the
University of Cambridge
to print and sell
all manner of books
was granted by
Henry VIII in 1534.
The University has printed
and published continuously
since 1584.

CAMBRIDGE UNIVERSITY PRESS

CAMBRIDGE

NEW YORK   PORT CHESTER   MELBOURNE   SYDNEY

Published by the Press Syndicate of the University of Cambridge
The Pitt Building, Trumpington Street, Cambridge CB2 1RP
40 West 20th Street, New York, NY 10011-4211, USA
10 Stamford Road, Oakleigh, Melbourne 3166, Australia

First published 1979
Reprinted 1981
Second edition 1991

Printed in Great Britain at the University Press, Cambridge

British Library Cataloguing in Publication Data

Cambridge problems in physics and advice on solutions. – 2nd
ed.
1. Physics
I. Dendy, P.P. (Philip Palin)   II. Tuffnell, R.   III. Mee, C.H.B.
IV. University of Cambridge Local Examinations Syndicate
530

ISBN 0 521 40956 X

Phototypeset at Thomson Press (India) Ltd., New Delhi

Contents

Contents

Guidance   **105**

Acknowledgements

These questions have been compiled by the editors on behalf of the University of Cambridge Local Examinations Syndicate. We would like to acknowledge our indebtedness to Dr K.E. Machin and Dr B. Elsmore, who originally devised some of the questions, and to Mr M.T.V. Hart, who prepared some of the notes for guidance. Suggestions for solutions are the opinions of the editors.

Preface

The ability to solve problems in physics does not follow naturally from any teaching course, however well delivered. Furthermore, worked examples and exercises in textbooks normally concentrate on the subject matter of a particular chapter, thus providing only limited experience for the student. It is thus not surprising to find that problem-solving is an area of physics that causes students particular difficulty. We have therefore gathered together a selection of questions that cover a wide range of physics at a level where we feel guidance is most necessary and likely to be of real benefit.

We have provided sufficient advice on methods of solution to enable students to improve their expertise in this vital aspect of physics. The advice has concentrated on those points in a question which are most likely to cause difficulty and has been written so as to leave some thinking for the student to do.

This particular collection of problems is based on questions set for the Special and 'STEP' Physics Papers by the University of Cambridge Local Examinations Syndicate during the years 1960–1989. One purpose of the Special Paper is to provide for the more gifted student of physics an objective that requires a deeper level of understanding than the normal higher school leaving examination (for example, the GCE Advanced Level). Similarly, the STEP Papers provide evidence for Cambridge College entrance. The book is therefore directed primarily at students who are preparing for these or similar examinations. In addition, many of the problems provide testing exercises for students who wish to study physics beyond the highest level generally taught at school, particularly 'HNC' or 'TEC' students in physics and applied physics, student teachers and, in many cases, first-year university students.

The questions are grouped under nine fairly conventional headings: general physics, physical quantities and measurement techniques; mechanics and gravitation; oscillations and waves, particularly light and sound; states of matter; heat and kinetic theory; electrostatics; current electricity; electromagnetism; and atomic and nuclear physics. Since, however, an important element of many of the problems is to show that physics is a coherent and integrated subject, the allocation is often only nominal and, in many questions, knowledge and understanding of several aspects of physics is required to give a full answer. The problems are somewhat variable in length, some consisting of examination questions in their original entirety with others being only (sometimes relatively short) extracts.

The questions are not constrained by any physics syllabus currently in use, but a full working knowledge of the language and terminology commonly associated with present-day GCE (Advanced Level) or HSC (Overseas) Physics syllabuses is assumed. SI units are used throughout, the symbolism being that adopted by the University of Cambridge Local Examinations Syndicate, i.e. in general conformity with the recommendations of the Association for Science Education. A summary of quantities, standard symbols and units—not to be considered exhaustive—is given after the Preface as a convenient reference list. This standard notation has been used throughout the book; and, in the 'guidance' sections, equations and quantities that the reader should readily recognise may be given in standard notation without defining the symbols. Physical quantities and constants that are specific to a given question are quoted within the question: however, in conformity with present practice, other standard and frequently used constants and values are given on page *xiv*. Within a group of questions on similar topics, an attempt has been made to order the questions in terms of difficulty. Where appropriate, there are cross-references to advice in other questions.

Students frequently meet the use of integration in physics problems for the first time at this stage, and a number of these problems require the solving of a definite integral. We have made no attempt to be mathematically too formal but have tried to distinguish between finite small displacements Δx and small displacements δx that may subsequently be assumed to be infinitesimal. To assist students who are not familiar with problems requiring integration, we have, in many cases, given the form of the integral, e.g. $\int kx^{-2}\,dx$, in terms of a non-specific variable x, which will remain to be identified in each problem. Questions or parts of questions involving integration, unless trivial, are marked with an asterisk: this symbol is also used where other points of physics are likely to be relatively more demanding.

Although these questions have been intensively vetted by students and teachers, errors in transcription and even occasionally inadequate physics may remain. We will welcome comments and criticisms from readers, particularly as regards any numerical errors in the answers. We would like to acknowledge our indebtedness to the various examiners who originally devised many of the questions. Suggestions for solutions are the opinions of the editors.

Summary of quantities, standard symbols and units

Quantity	Usual symbols	Usual unit
Base quantities		
mass	m	kg
length	l	m
time	t	s
electric current	I	A
thermodynamic temperature	T	K
amount of substance	n	mol
Other quantities		
acceleration, deceleration	$a, \ddot{x}, \ldots$	$\mathrm{m\,s^{-2}}$
acceleration of free fall	g	$\mathrm{m\,s^{-2}}$
activity of radioactive source	A	$\mathrm{s^{-1}}$
amplitude	A	m
angle of contact	θ	° (degrees)
angular acceleration	$\dot{\omega}, \ddot{\theta}$	$\mathrm{rad\,s^{-2}}$
angular frequency $(2\pi f)$	ω	$\mathrm{rad\,s^{-1}}$
angular momentum	p_θ, b, L	$\mathrm{kg\,m^2\,rad\,s^{-1}}$
angular velocity	$\omega, \Omega, \dot{\theta}$	$\mathrm{rad\,s^{-1}}$
area	A, S	$\mathrm{m^2}$
atomic mass unit	m_u	kg
Avogadro constant	L, N_A	$\mathrm{mol^{-1}}$
Boltzmann constant	k	$\mathrm{J\,K^{-1}}$
bulk modulus	K	Pa
capacitance	C	F
charge	q, Q	C
coefficient of friction	μ	—
conductance	G	$\mathrm{S} = \Omega^{-1}$
conductivity	σ	$\mathrm{S\,m^{-1}} = \Omega^{-1}\,\mathrm{m^{-1}}$
couple (see also torque)	T	N m
critical angle	θ_c	° (degrees)
current density	J, j	$\mathrm{A\,m^{-2}}$
decay constant	λ	$\mathrm{s^{-1}}$

Summary of quantities, standard symbols and units

density	ρ	$\text{kg}\,\text{m}^{-3}$
diameter	d, D	m
displacement	d, s	m
distance	d, s	m
efficiency	η	–
electric charge	Q	C
electric field strength	E	$\text{V}\,\text{m}^{-1}$
electric potential	V, ϕ	V
electromotive force, e.m.f.	E	V
electron mass	m_e	kg
energy	E	J
electron volt	–	eV
expansivity, cubic	β	K^{-1}
expansivity, linear	α	K^{-1}
focal length	f	m
force	$F, \mathbf{F}$	N
force constant	k	$\text{N}\,\text{m}^{-1}$
free path	λ	m
frequency	ν, f	Hz
gravitational constant	G	$\text{N}\,\text{m}^2\,\text{kg}^{-2}$
gravitational field	g	$\text{N}\,\text{kg}^{-1} = \text{m}\,\text{s}^{-2}$
gravitational potential	Φ	$\text{J}\,\text{kg}^{-1}$
half-life	$T_{1/2}, t_{1/2}$	s
Hall coefficient	R_{H}	$\text{m}^3\,\text{C}^{-1}$
heat capacity	C	$\text{J}\,\text{K}^{-1}$
illumination (luminous flux)	F	lx
image distance	v	m
impedance	Z	Ω
impulse	J	N s
intensity	I	$\text{W}\,\text{m}^{-2}$
kinetic energy	T, K, E_{k}	J
latent heat	L	J
magnetic field intensity	H	$\text{A}\,\text{m}^{-1}$
magnetic flux	Φ	Wb
magnetic flux density	B	T
magnifying power	M	–
molar gas constant	R	$\text{J}\,\text{K}^{-1}\,\text{mol}^{-1}$
molar heat capacity	C_{m}	$\text{J}\,\text{K}^{-1}\,\text{mol}^{-1}$
molar mass	M	$\text{kg}\,\text{mol}^{-1}$
moment of inertia	I	$\text{kg}\,\text{m}^2$
momentum	$p, \mathbf{P}$	$\text{kg}\,\text{m}\,\text{s}^{-1}$
mutual inductance	M, L_{12}	H
neutron mass	m_{n}	kg
normal stress	σ	Pa
number per unit volume	n	m^{-3}
object distance	u	m
order (of diffraction)	n	–
period	T	s
permeability	μ	$\text{H}\,\text{m}^{-1}$

Summary of quantities, standard symbols and units

permeability of free space	μ_0	$H\,m^{-1}$
permittivity	ε	$F\,m^{-1}$
permittivity of free space	ε_0	$F\,m^{-1}$
phase angle	ϕ	rad
Planck constant	h	J s
potential difference	V	V
potential energy	V, Φ, E_p	J
power	P	W
power factor	$\cos\phi$	–
pressure	p	Pa
principal molar heat capacities	$C_{V,m}, C_{p,m}$	$J\,K^{-1}\,mol^{-1}$
proton mass	m_p	kg
radius	r, a	m
ratio of principal heat capacities	γ	–
reactance	X	Ω
refractive index	n	–
relative atomic mass	A_r	–
relative molecular mass	M_r	–
relative permeability	μ_r	–
relative permittivity	ε_r	–
resistance	R	Ω
resistivity	ρ	$\Omega\,m$
self-inductance	L	H
shear stress	τ	Pa
specific charge	q	$C\,kg^{-1}$
specific heat capacity	c	$J\,K^{-1}\,kg^{-1}$
specific latent heat	l	$J\,kg^{-1}$
speed	$u, v, w, \dot{x}, \ldots$	$m\,s^{-1}$
speed of electromagnetic waves	c	$m\,s^{-1}$
Stefan constant	σ	$W\,m^{-2}\,K^{-4}$
strain	ε	–
stress	σ	Pa
surface tension	γ, σ	$N\,m^{-1}$
temperature	t, θ	°C
temperature coefficient of resistance	α	$K^{-1}, (°C)^{-1}$
tension	T	N
thermal conductivity	k, λ	$W\,m^{-1}\,K^{-1}$
time constant	τ	s
torque	T	N m
triple point	T_{tr}	K
unified atomic mass constant	m_u	kg
velocity	$u, v, w, \dot{x}, \ldots$	$m\,s^{-1}$
viscosity	η	Pa s
volume	V, v	m^3
wavelength	λ	m
work, energy	W, E, U	J
work function	ϕ	V
Young modulus	E	Pa

Summary of quantities, standard symbols and units

Other symbols

average of x	$\langle x \rangle$
greater than	$>$
less than	$<$
arbitrary zero	(subscript)$_0$
infinity	∞
proportional to	$\propto$
approximately equal to	$\approx$

Physics constants

speed of light in a vacuum	c	$= 3.00 \times 10^8 \, \mathrm{m\,s^{-1}}$
permeability of a vacuum	μ_0	$= 4\pi \times 10^{-7} \, \mathrm{H\,m^{-1}}$
permittivity of a vacuum	ε_0	$= 8.85 \times 10^{-12} \, \mathrm{F\,m^{-1}}$
		$\approx (1/(36\pi)) \times 10^{-9} \, \mathrm{F\,m^{-1}}$
electronic charge	e	$= -1.60 \times 10^{-19} \, \mathrm{C}$
Planck constant	h	$= 6.63 \times 10^{-34} \, \mathrm{J\,s}$
unified atomic mass constant	u	$= 1.66 \times 10^{-27} \, \mathrm{kg}$
rest mass of electron	m_e	$= 9.11 \times 10^{-31} \, \mathrm{kg}$
rest mass of proton	m_p	$= 1.67 \times 10^{-27} \, \mathrm{kg}$
molar gas constant	R	$= 8.31 \, \mathrm{J\,K^{-1}\,mol^{-1}}$
Avogadro constant	L	$= 6.02 \times 10^{23} \, \mathrm{mol^{-1}}$
Boltzmann constant	k	$= 1.38 \times 10^{-23} \, \mathrm{J\,K^{-1}}$
gravitational constant	G	$= 6.67 \times 10^{-11} \, \mathrm{N\,m^2\,kg^{-2}}$
acceleration of free fall	g	$= 9.81 \, \mathrm{m\,s^{-2}}$

Problems

Section G

General physics, physical quantities and measurement techniques

G1 Determine from dimensional considerations which of the following relations are incorrect, given that the constants k are dimensionless.

(a) Force required to cause collapse of a strut of circular cross-section

$$= k_1 \times \frac{(\text{Young modulus}) \times (\text{radius})^4}{(\text{length})^2}.$$

(b) Couple required to rotate a gyroscope about an axis PQ at right angles to that of its rotor

$= k_2 \times (\text{moment of inertia of rotor}) \times (\text{angular velocity of rotor}) \times (\text{angular velocity about PQ}).$

(c) Power of single-cylinder steam engine

$= k_3 \times (\text{pressure of steam}) \times (\text{length of stroke of piston}) \times (\text{diameter of cylinder}) \times (\text{number of revolutions of shaft per minute}).$

(d) Maximum number of skittles that may be knocked over by a single ball

$$= k_4 \times \frac{(\text{mass of ball}) \times (\text{speed of ball})^2}{(\text{mass of skittle}) \times (\text{height of centre of gravity of skittle})}.$$

Are those relations that you did not find to be incorrect necessarily correct? Give reasons.

G2 (a) According to quantum theory, the radius r of the hydrogen atom should be controlled by the quantities e, ε_0, h and m, being the elementary charge, the permittivity of free space, the Planck constant and the electron mass, respectively.

Write down or deduce the dimensions of these quantities, and use them to find a dimensionally correct expression for *r*. Assuming that the dimensionless constant in this expression is 1, calculate the value of *r*. Comment on your result.

(b) There are some relationships that cannot be found using dimensional analysis. One of these is the expression for the force *F* acting on a disc of radius *R* placed normal to the flow in a fluid of density ρ and viscosity η, when the speed of the fluid when unperturbed by the disc is *v*. Given that the dimensions of viscosity are $M\,L^{-1}\,T^{-1}$, explain why dimensional analysis cannot give an expression for *F* in terms of R, ρ, η and *v*. In practice, such cases may often be dealt with by identifying dimensionless combinations of variables. Find two independent dimensionless combinations from among the variables F, R, ρ, η and *v*.

G3   The intensity *I* of an electromagnetic wave in vacuum is related to the peak value E_0 of the electric field vector associated with the wave by the quation

$$I = \varepsilon_0 E_0^2 c/2,$$

where ε_0 is the permittivity of a vacuum and *c* is the speed of light. Write down an SI unit for each of the quantities in this equation. Hence show that the equation is dimensionally correct.

A certain helium–neon laser emits 0.2 mW in a beam of cross-sectional area 3 mm^2. Estimate the peak value of the electric field vector associated with this laser beam.

G4   The speed *v* of surface waves of wavelength λ on a liquid of density ρ is given by

$$v = [(a\lambda/2\pi) + (2\pi b/\rho\lambda)]^{1/2},$$

where *a* is a constant and *b* is a quantity characteristic of the liquid. Determine the dimensions (or SI base units) of *a* and *b*.

Surface water waves of wavelength 20.0 mm have a speed of 0.230 m s^{-1} at room temperature. At about 50 °C, the speed of waves of the same wavelength is 0.225 m s^{-1}. Assuming that the density of water remains unchanged at 1.00×10^3 kg m^{-3}, estimate the change in the quantity *b* between these two temperatures.

G5   The following experiment is carried out to check the shutter speed of a camera. Point sources of light P and Q are fixed at the centre and at a point on the circumference of the turntable of a record player (Fig. G5.1).

The camera is focused on the rotating turntable and a photo-

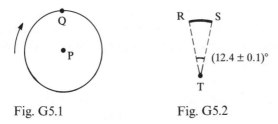

Fig. G5.1   Fig. G5.2

graph is taken with a nominal exposure time of 1/15 s. When the film is developed, an arc RS and a spot T appear on the negative (Fig. G5.2). The arc subtends an angle of 12.4° at the point T. The uncertainty in this measurement is ±0.1°. The speed of the turntable is known to be (33.3 ± 0.1) revolutions per minute. What can you deduce about the actual exposure time?

G6   The position of a particle is given by

$$x = a \sin \omega t, \qquad y = a \cos \omega t, \qquad z = bt.$$

Find the magnitude of the velocity and of the acceleration of the particle at time t. Find also the angle between the velocity and acceleration vectors.

Draw a sketch of the path of the particle and describe its motion.

G7   Two interacting particles of mass m_1 and m_2 are constrained to move in the x direction only. Their positions are given by x_1 and x_2 at time t. Obtain an expression for X_0, the position of their centre of mass, at this instant.

Three identical interacting particles A, B and C are constrained to move in the x, y plane and are acted upon by a constant external force. Their position coordinates at various times are as follows:

	Coordinate		
Time	A	B	C
0	(1, 1)	(2, 2)	(3, 3)
later	(1, 0)	(0, 1)	(3, 3)
later still	(0, 1)	(1, 2)	(2, 0)

Determine the direction in which the force is acting.

G8   A car is travelling at speed v along a straight level road towards a gate that may close automatically at any time. A visual warning is given a short period T before the gate closes. The car's maximum deceleration under braking is a. Show that there is a maximum safe speed, given by $v_{max} = 2Ta$, above which the car may be able neither to stop nor to pass (without accelerating) before the gate closes.

Calculate a suitable value for T if $a = 3.0\,\mathrm{m\,s^{-2}}$ and speeds up to $30\,\mathrm{m\,s^{-1}}$ are to be safe.

G9 The practical value of a device for storing energy can be assessed by the height to which it would rise if all the stored energy were used to propel it upwards. Calculate this height for the following:

(a) a 12 V car battery of capacity 60 A h and mass 20 kg;

(b) a $1.0\,\mu\mathrm{F}$ capacitor of mass 100 g charged to 5.0 kV;

(c) a quantity of petrol of calorific value $4 \times 10^7\,\mathrm{J\,kg^{-1}}$;

(d) a spring of mass 200 g stretched a distance of 10 cm by a force of 100 N.

G10 Describe briefly what you understand by *stable* and *unstable* equilibria of a system.

(a) A sphere rests inside a fixed rough hemispherical bowl of twice its radius. A mass M is attached at the highest point of the sphere. Discuss the stability of the sphere.

(b) An amplifier is connected with a microphone at its input and a loudspeaker at the output. Discuss the stability of the system when the microphone is placed near the loudspeaker.

G11 A solid metal cylinder is placed in frictionless bearings and set to rotate about its axis. Without further mechanical contact, the cylinder is then heated until its diameter has increased by 0.16%. Given that the moment of inertia of a solid cylinder is proportional to the square of its radius, find the percentage changes in (a) the angular momentum, (b) the angular velocity and (c) the energy of rotation of the cylinder.

Comment on the energy changes that occur in the system.

G12 Measurements of electrical conductivity and Hall voltage for a sample of pure semiconductor show that n, the charge carrier concentration per unit volume, increases rapidly with temperature. A simple theory to explain this rapid increase in n leads to the prediction that

$$n = n_0 \exp(-E/2kT),$$

where E is a measure of the energy an electron requires before it can take part in the conduction process, T is the thermodynamic temperature, n_0 is a constant and k is the Boltzmann constant.

Measurements of n as a function of T gave the following results:

n/m^{-3}	6.31×10^{17}	3.98×10^{19}	2.51×10^{20}	2.00×10^{21}
T/K	250	300	350	400
n/m^{-3}	2.51×10^{22}	3.30×10^{23}	4.03×10^{24}	
T/K	500	700	1000	

Plot a graph to investigate the extent to which the data support the simple model and obtain a value for E.

G13 In a certain experiment to investigate the quantum yield γ (electrons per incident photon) in photoemission, the following results were obtained:

Photon energy, E/eV	4.2	4.3	4.4	4.5	4.6	4.7	4.8
$\gamma/10^{-6}$	0.009	0.372	1.267	2.704	4.651	7.140	10.120

Draw a graph of γ against E and hence deduce an approximate value for E_0, the work function of the emitter.

A theory suggests that γ varies with E according to an expression of the form

$$\gamma = A(E - E_0)^n,$$

where A is a constant and n is an integer. Using your approximate value of E_0, deduce the most likely value of n, and hence find an accurate value for E_0.

G14 What do you understand by a *frame of reference*? Illustrate your answer by explaining what is meant (a) when an observer of a train says 'the train is travelling at 60 miles per hour', (b) by the words 'up' and 'down'.

A smooth, flat, horizontal turntable 4.0 m in diameter is rotating at 0.05 revolutions per second. A student, who is at the centre of the turntable and rotating with it, reaches out and carefully places a smooth flat disc on the turntable, 0.5 m from the edge.

Describe the behaviour of the disc as seen by his colleague who is standing at the side of the turntable. How long does the disc remain on the turntable?

What would the student on the turntable see happening to the disc? In which direction would he see the disc travelling when it leaves the edge? How might this student explain the behaviour of the disc if he were unaware of his own rotation?

Section M

Mechanics and gravitation

M1 The net force F resisting the motion of a cyclist travelling at speed v along a level road, in still air, may be described by the equation

$$F = Av^2 + B,$$

where A and B are constants.

The following table gives experimental data on the power P developed by the cyclist on a level road, in still air, as a function of the speed.

$v/\mathrm{m\,s}^{-1}$	1.4	3.2	4.7	6.5	8.5	9.8	11.2	12.1
P/W	6	19	37	82	149	224	298	373

(a) By drawing a suitable graph, use these data to estimate the constants A and B.

(b) The cyclist can sustain a power of 60 W over long periods. By plotting a suitable curve on your graph, and finding the point of intersection, or otherwise, determine the maximum speed that the cyclist can sustain on a level road, in still air.

(c) Suggest what is meant by each of the terms Av^2 and B.

M2 *Implosion* is a possible hazard when using glass apparatus that has been evacuated: that is, if the glass breaks, it is projected inwards. Suppose such an accident occurs to the tube of a domestic television set. Make suitable numerical estimates of the size of the tube and any other quantities that you need to obtain approximate values of the following:

(a) the force exerted by the atmosphere on the screen of the tube before the implosion takes place;

(b) the energy released in the implosion;

(c) the initial speed of the fragments of glass.

You should indicate clearly the physical principles you have used for each calculation.

M3 A small sphere is released from rest and, after falling a vertical distance of 0.5 m, bounces on a smooth plane that is inclined at 10° to the horizontal. If the sphere loses no energy during the impact, why do its directions of motion immediately before and immediately after the impact make equal angles with the normal to the plane?

Find the distance, measured down the plane, between this impact and the next.

M4 The motors of a rocket launched from the Earth are used only near the Earth in order to give the rocket just sufficient energy to reach the Moon. Find where, subsequently, the velocity of the rocket is a minimum and calculate the speed with which it hits the Moon's surface (the motion of the Moon may be neglected).

	Mass/kg	Radius/km
Earth	6.0×10^{24}	6.4×10^{3}
Moon	7.3×10^{22}	1.7×10^{3}

[Earth–Moon distance $= 3.8 \times 10^5$ km.]

M5 In order to send a space vehicle to the Moon, it is usual first to place the vehicle in a circular 'parking orbit' near to the Earth, and then to increase its speed in an appropriate direction so that it escapes from the influence of the Earth and becomes a satellite of the Moon.

(a) Determine the speed v of the vehicle when it is in parking orbit close to the surface of the Earth.

(b) Describe how, if at all, the rotation of the Earth affects the energy required to place the vehicle in the parking orbit.

(c)* In the parking orbit, friction with the outer layers of the Earth's atmosphere causes a gradual reduction in total energy, but it is observed that the vehicle actually moves faster. Explain this apparent paradox.

(d) A long way from the Moon, the vehicle has a speed of $0.50 \, \text{km s}^{-1}$ and, if it continued along this trajectory, it would miss the centre of the Moon by a distance X. Neglecting the effect of the Earth, determine the value of X so that it just avoids hitting the surface of the Moon. Find, also, its speed at the point of closest approach to the Moon.

(e) The speed required for a parking orbit close to the surface of the Moon is $1.7 \, \text{km s}^{-1}$. Describe how and when the vehicle can be put into this new parking orbit, given that the mass of the vehicle is $50\,000 \, \text{kg}$ and that rocket motors on the vehicle have an available thrust of $8.0 \times 10^5 \, \text{N}$.

[Mass of Earth $= 6.0 \times 10^{24} \, \text{kg}$; radius of Earth $= 6.4 \times 10^6 \, \text{m}$; period of rotation of Earth $= 8.6 \times 10^4 \, \text{s}$; mass of Moon $= 7.3 \times 10^{22} \, \text{kg}$; radius of Moon $= 1.7 \times 10^6 \, \text{m}$.]

M6 A space-research rocket stands vertically on its launching pad. Prior to ignition, the mass of the rocket and its fuel is $4.1 \times 10^3 \, \text{kg}$. On ignition, gas is ejected from the rocket at a speed of $2.5 \times 10^3 \, \text{m s}^{-1}$ relative to the rocket, and fuel is consumed at a constant rate of $16 \, \text{kg s}^{-1}$. Show that the rocket does not leave the pad immediately. Calculate the time interval between ignition and lift-off.

M7 A bag containing a mass M of sand is suspended from a hook on the arm of a balance at a height h above the balance pan. At a time $t = 0$, the sand starts to pour from a hole at the bottom of the bag, falling onto the pan beneath, and continues at a constant rate r (mass/unit time) until the bag is empty.

Find the mass required on the other pan to maintain balance under steady conditions when a continuous stream of sand is falling from the bag (a simple balance with equal arms is envisaged).

Show graphically the variation with time of the mass required to maintain balance throughout the experiment, indicating by suitable labelling the quantities involved. Assume ideal conditions, under which air resistance, balance inertia and damping effects may be ignored.

M8 A uniform chain of mass M and length L is hung vertically with its lower end just touching a table top and is then allowed to fall freely. After time t, a length l of the chain is lying on the table top. Show that the force F exerted by the chain on the table is given by

$$F = Mgl/L + Mg^2t^2/L.$$

Derive an expression in terms of M and g for F', the value of F at the moment when the top of the chain reaches the table.

Draw a graph to show how F varies with t.

M9 (a) A body moving through a liquid may experience a retarding force because of turbulent disturbance of the liquid. The magnitude of the force depends upon the speed, size and shape of the body.

Consider a body moving through a liquid of density ρ with uniform velocity v under turbulent conditions. The cross-sectional area of the body at right angles to the direction of motion is A. The body pushes a certain volume of liquid out of the way in unit time and it can be assumed that, after it has been pushed out of the way, this liquid moves with velocity v in the same direction as the body.

  (i) By considering the rate of change of momentum of this liquid, show that the retarding force acting on the body is $Av^2\rho$. Refer clearly to the physical principles involved.

  (ii) Experimentally, it is found that the retarding force is given by $KAv^2\rho$, where K is a constant that depends on the shape of the body and is always less than 1. Explain why you might expect the value of K to be less than 1.

(b) An aerator nozzle is fitted 0.40 m below the surface of the water in a fish tank. It is noted that air bubbles from the nozzle accelerate upwards for the first few millimetres of their motion but then rise to the surface with a constant terminal speed. For bubbles of diameter 3.0 mm, this speed is found to be $0.31\,\mathrm{m\,s^{-1}}$. The passage of the bubbles through the water is turbulent.

  (i) Explain why the bubbles first accelerate and then come to move with a constant terminal speed.

  (ii) Deduce the value of the constant K in the expression for the retarding force due to turbulence in this system.

     [Take the density of water as $1.0 \times 10^3\,\mathrm{kg\,m^{-3}}$ and the density of air in the bubbles as $1.3\,\mathrm{kg\,m^{-3}}$.]

  (iii) As the bubbles rise, the pressure due to the water above them decreases. Estimate the resulting fractional change in the radius of a bubble as it rises from the nozzle to the surface. Discuss whether this change makes a significant difference to the terminal speed.

M10   Show that the final kinetic energy E of a neutron after a head-on elastic collision with a stationary nucleus of nucleon (mass) number A is given by $E = E_0[(A-1)/(A+1)]^2$, where E_0 is the initial neutron kinetic energy.

On the basis of this calculation, state with reasons which types of material you consider most suitable for neutron shielding.

Assuming that the above expression describes all collisions of a neutron in a graphite moderator at room temperature, estimate the number of collisions required to reduce a 3 MeV neutron to that energy at which it is in thermal equilibrium with its surroundings.

Calculate an approximate value for the de Broglie wavelength of a thermal neutron.

[Relative atomic mass, A_r, of carbon is 12; $1\,\mathrm{eV} = 1.6 \times 10^{-19}\,\mathrm{J}$.]

M11 An aircraft flies due east along the Equator at a constant altitude and a steady speed relative to the ground. An observer in the aircraft suspends a mass on a sensitive spring balance and records a value W_1. When the aircraft flies due west along the Equator at the same altitude and speed relative to the ground, the balance reading is W_2. Why is there a difference between W_1 and W_2?

Suppose the mass used in the experiment is 1.0 kg and the speed of the aircraft (measured at the height of the aircraft) is 200 m s^{-1}. How sensitive must the balance be to detect the difference between W_1 and W_2?

M12 Fig. M12.1 shows a section through a smooth metal bowl, which can be rotated about its axis Oy. The equation of this section, related to the axes Ox and Oy, is $y = ax^2$, where a is a constant; the gradient of the tangent to the curve at the point P(x, y) is $2ax$.

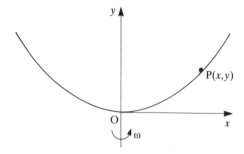

Fig. M12.1

It is found that there is one particular speed of rotation ω for which a small metal sphere remains at rest relative to the rotating bowl, wherever it is placed on the inner surface. Find an expression for the critical angular speed ω in terms of a and g, the acceleration of free fall.

If a larger sphere of radius r (no longer negligible compared with the dimensions of the bowl) were used, determine whether the angular speed for dynamic equilibrium is still independent of the position of the sphere in the bowl.

M13 A particle is placed 10 cm from the centre of a rough turntable. The turntable is steadily accelerated at 20 rad s^{-2}. When the angular velocity reaches 7.0 rad s^{-1}, the particle starts to slip. If the particle had originally been placed 15 cm from the centre and the turntable accelerated as before, at what angular velocity would it have started to slip?

M14 Fan blades of radius r are mounted directly on the axle of a d.c. electric motor. Assuming that the fan imparts a velocity v to a cylinder of air of radius equal to that of the blades, and that the density of the air is ρ, obtain expressions for:

(a) the rate at which momentum is transferred to the air,

(b) the thrust on the motor,

(c) the rate of working of the motor,

(d) the rate at which kinetic energy is supplied to the air.

Comment on any apparent conflict between your answers.

Calculate the velocity of the air in the following case: motor voltage $= 24\,\mathrm{V}$; current $= 1.2\,\mathrm{A}$; efficiency $= 80\%$; diameter of fan blades $= 30\,\mathrm{cm}$; density of air $= 1.2\,\mathrm{kg\,m^{-3}}$.

M15 (a) Two stars separated by a large distance d rotate in circular orbits about their common centre of mass. Given that one star has a mass m and the other a mass $2m$, find an expression for their period of rotation in terms of d, m and G, the universal gravitational constant.

(b) Show that the total kinetic energy of the system is numerically equal to one-half of its gravitational potential energy but of opposite sign.

(c) Taking m as $3 \times 10^{30}\,\mathrm{kg}$, d as $1 \times 10^{11}\,\mathrm{m}$ and the double star system to be receding at $2 \times 10^{6}\,\mathrm{m\,s^{-1}}$, describe in detail what would be seen if continuous observations were made of a spectral line that has a wavelength of $434.05\,\mathrm{nm}$ as measured in the laboratory. You may assume the observer to be in the plane of orbit of the stars.

M16 Estimate the theoretical maximum power available from the following systems for energy production:

(a) a windmill of sail area $30\,\mathrm{m^2}$ when the wind speed is (i) $10\,\mathrm{m\,s^{-1}}$, (ii) $20\,\mathrm{m\,s^{-1}}$;

(b) a tidal energy scheme with a tidal basin area of $50\,\mathrm{km^2}$ and a tidal rise and fall of $10\,\mathrm{m}$ every $6\,\mathrm{h}$.

Surplus energy from an electricity generating station is to be stored by pumping water into an elevated reservoir. Give estimates for the necessary dimensions of the reservoir (height, surface area and depth) if it is to be capable of storing 75% of the output over a $12\,\mathrm{h}$ period from a $1.8\,\mathrm{GW}$ station. Comment on the estimates you have given.

[Density of air $= 1.2\,\mathrm{kg\,m^{-3}}$; density of water $= 1.0 \times 10^{3}\,\mathrm{kg\,m^{-3}}$.]

M17* A body is travelling in a circular orbit of radius r under the influence of a force that is directed towards the centre of the circle and is proportional to $1/r^{n}$. By considering the effect of a small increase in radius to $(r + dr)$, or otherwise, show that the orbit is unstable if $n \geqslant 3$.

M18 It is required to put a satellite into a circular orbit just above the Earth's surface. If the radius of the Earth is taken to be 6400 km, with what speed should the satellite be launched?

If the satellite is launched from Cambridge (latitude 52° 10′) and the orbit is to pass directly over the north pole, in what direction should it be launched?

[Ignore atmospheric effects.]

M19* If you inhabited a 'flat earth' consisting of a large stationary disc of rock of uniform thickness X and known density ρ, how could you deduce its thickness from measurements of g just above the surface near the central region?

M20* Describe how you would measure the acceleration of free fall, g, to an accuracy of about 0.5%.

Would the value you obtained be different if the floor of your laboratory, which may be considered to be large, were covered with a layer of lead 1 m thick?

[Density of lead, $\rho = 11.2 \times 10^3 \, \text{kg m}^{-3}$. You may, if you wish, use the fact that the force due to an annular ring of mass m per unit area acting on unit mass at a point P on the axis of the ring is $2\pi Gm \sin\theta \, \delta\theta$, where θ and $(\theta + \delta\theta)$ are the angles subtended at P by the radii of the annular ring.]

M21 Show that, if a large mass M, moving with velocity V, makes a head-on elastic collision with a very small stationary mass m, the energy lost by the large mass is approximately $2mV^2$.

The large mass passes through a gas of density ρ. If the mass presents a cross-section of area A to the gas molecules (which may be treated as being stationary), show that the rate of loss of energy of the mass is $2A\rho V^3$. Hence, or otherwise, derive an expression for the time for the velocity of the mass to be reduced by a half.

M22* A spherical star of uniform density ρ and radius R is formed by the condensation of interstellar dust from large distances due to gravitational forces. Find the energy change that occurs at some intermediate stage as the radius increases from r to $r + \delta r$.

Hence derive an expression in terms of the gravitational constant G, R and the mass M of the star for the total loss of gravitational energy during the condensation.

M23 Values of the gravitational potential V at different distances d from the centre of the Earth are given below. The radius of the Earth is 6400 km.

d/km	6400	6700	8100	10 100	13 400	20 200	40 300	∞
V/MJ kg^{-1}	-63	-60	-50	-40	-30	-20	-10	0

Using the above data, where appropriate, answer the following.
   (a) Find the acceleration of free fall near the Earth's surface.
   (b) Determine the total energy required to move a satellite of mass 2000 kg from a stable orbit just above the Earth's surface to one at altitude 7000 km.
   (c) Calculate the difference in gravitational field strength between the top of Mount Everest (8000 m above sea level) and sea level.
   (d)* Assuming the Earth to be a uniform sphere, show that the gravitational field strength decreases uniformly with depth below the surface and is zero at the centre of the Earth.
   (e) Estimate the precision that would be required if this prediction is to be tested by measurements of gravitational field strength in available mine shafts.
   (f) Explain why the mean sea level can be up to 1 m higher above oil-bearing rock than above non-oil-bearing rock, which is usually denser.

M24* A rocket that is to be launched vertically has a total mass of 1.0×10^5 kg, of which 0.8×10^5 kg is fuel. The fuel is to be burned at a constant rate of 800 kg s^{-1}. What is the minimum velocity of burnt fuel, relative to the rocket, that will allow lift-off at the start of burn?
   If the actual velocity of the burnt fuel, relative to the rocket, is 1.5×10^3 m s^{-1} at all times, what is the maximum acceleration of the rocket and when does this occur?
   [Neglect air resistance. Take g as 10 m s^{-2}, and neglect any variation of g with height.]
   Why are multi-stage rockets used rather than single-stage rockets?

M25 A metal cylinder of cross-sectional area A contains a fixed mass of an ideal gas, confined by a smoothly fitting piston. The piston may be moved by applying a force F through a spring of force constant k, as shown in Fig. M25.1.
   Initially, when the piston is at a distance y_0 from the closed end of the cylinder, the enclosed gas is at atmospheric pressure p_0 and is in thermal equilibrium with the surroundings. The force F is increased from zero and the piston moves outwards very slowly, so that thermal equilibrium is maintained.

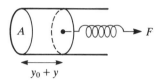

Fig. M25.1

(a) Find an expression for the force F when the piston has moved a distance y from the original position.

(b) For the case in which the gas is expanded to three times its initial volume, find the work done by the gas in expanding, and the work done in stretching the spring.

M26* The turntable of a record player has moment of inertia I about its spindle. It is rotating at an angular speed of Ω when the drive is cut off. The turntable is slowed down by a frictional torque T that is proportional to the angular speed ω; that is, $T = k\omega$, where k is a constant.

(a) Find an expression for the angular speed of the turntable at any time t after the drive is disconnected.

(b) Sketch a graph of the variation of ω with t.

(c) At what time does $\omega = \Omega/2$? How could you deduce from your graph the number of revolutions made by the turntable in this time? Show that this number is $I\Omega/4\pi k$.

Section W

Oscillations and waves, particularly light and sound

W1 A camera, which has a lens of focal length 5.0 cm and diameter of 2.0 cm, takes a photograph of a 100 W filament lamp 100 m away. If 1% of the energy is emitted as visible light and the exposure lasts 0.015 s, estimate the number of photons with wavelengths in the visible range that strike the film.

W2 Suggest explanations for the following, giving any calculations you think are relevant.

(a) Coloured objects frequently look different when viewed in artificial light than in daylight.

(b) Interference effects may easily be obtained with two identical laser sources of yellow light but not easily using two separate sodium discharge lamps.

(c) A slit 0.1 mm wide will produce appreciable diffraction effects with visible light but not when 10 keV electrons behave as waves.

(d) A beam of unpolarised light is stopped completely by two crossed sheets of polaroid. If a third sheet of polaroid is inserted between the other two and rotated at frequency f about the optical axis, light is transmitted by the complete system and its intensity fluctuates at a frequency other than f.

[Wavelength of yellow light = 600 nm.]

W3 A simple pendulum, consisting of a mass m on the end of a string of length l, performs simple harmonic oscillations of angular amplitude θ. Derive from first principles an expression for the period. What would be the period:

(a) in a lift ascending with uniform acceleration a,

(b) in a lorry travelling at a constant speed v round the arc of a horizontal circle of radius r?

Would the periods in (a) and (b) be greater or less if the amplitude were large? Explain your reasoning.

If $m = 0.20\,\text{kg}$, $l = 1.5\,\text{m}$ and the pendulum is set swinging in the laboratory with $\theta = 5.0°$, calculate the maximum and minimum tensions in the string.

W4 A mass M is performing small vertical oscillations on the end of a light vertical spring. Show from first principles that the total energy of this motion at any instant in time can be written as $Ma^2\omega^2/2$, and identify the symbols.

If the mass M collides elastically, when it is travelling with maximum velocity, with a stationary body, which is of mass $M/2$ and is free to move, what is the new amplitude of the motion of mass M?

Explain, without attempting to solve the relevant equations, how the answer would be modified if the two masses had stuck together.

W5 Show that the average kinetic energy of a body of mass m vibrating with simple harmonic motion with amplitude A at frequency $\omega/2\pi$ is $m\omega^2 A^2/4$.

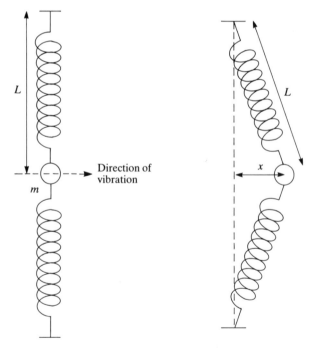

Fig. W5.1   Fig. W5.2

A small mass m is suspended between two fixed points by stretched springs of length L, as shown in Fig. W5.1. Each spring exerts a tension T.

If the mass is given a small lateral displacement x in the direction shown in Fig. W5.2, and assuming no change in the tension or the length of the spring when the mass is displaced, show that the mass executes simple harmonic motion. What is the frequency of oscillation if the mass is 10 g, the length of each stretched spring is 10 cm and the tension in each spring is 15 N?

The above example can be taken as a very simple model of the way the human eardrum responds to a sound wave, which causes it to vibrate with simple harmonic motion at the same frequency as the sound. A sound wave of frequency $\omega/2\pi$ and amplitude A travelling at speed v in air of density ρ has an intensity I given by

$$I = \rho\omega^2 A^2 v/2.$$

Show that the average kinetic energy E_k of the vibrating eardrum is given by

$$E_k = mI/2\rho v,$$

where m is the mass of the vibrating eardrum.

The human ear can respond to sound wave intensities down to about $1 \times 10^{-12}\,\mathrm{W\,m^{-2}}$. At this intensity, determine

(a) the average kinetic energy of the eardrum,

(b) the amplitude of oscillation of the eardrum when the frequency is 1 kHz.

[You may assume that the eardrum oscillates at the same frequency and with the same amplitude as the incident sound wave.]

Comment on your answers in relation to the kinetic energy of the eardrum due to random molecular bombardment ($\approx 6 \times 10^{-21}\,\mathrm{J}$) and the diameter of the hydrogen atom ($\approx 5 \times 10^{-11}\,\mathrm{m}$).

[Density of air $= 1.3\,\mathrm{kg\,m^{-3}}$; speed of sound in air $= 330\,\mathrm{m\,s^{-1}}$; mass of eardrum $= 1 \times 10^{-4}\,\mathrm{kg}$.]

W6 (a) In the kitchen weighing machine shown in Fig. W6.1, a scale pan is displaced downwards against a spring. The displacement x is indicated by a pointer. When an object of mass M is placed in the scale pan, the equilibrium displacement is αM, where α is a constant.

The object is held in contact with the pan with $x = 0$ and released at time $t = 0$.

Show that the object executes simple harmonic motion. Find the maximum reading of the pointer (in terms of M) and the time at which this reading first occurs. (Neglect friction and the inertia of the moving parts of the machine.)

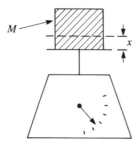

Fig. W6.1

(b) A more sophisticated machine, also commonly found in kitchens, contains two springs. The effect of these is that the machine is more sensitive to masses less than some fixed value M_0 than it is to greater masses. The equilibrium displacement is $\alpha_1 M$ when $M < M_0$, and $(\alpha_2 M + c)$ when $M > M_0$, where α_1, α_2 and c are constants.

An object of mass M_0 is held in contact with the pan with $x = 0$ and released at $t = 0$. Describe, with the aid of a sketch graph, the subsequent periodic motion. Find an expression for the period, and show that the maximum reading of the pointer is given by

$$M_0[1 + (\alpha_1/\alpha_2)^{1/2}].$$

W7 A body of mass m is free to slide on a smooth horizontal table and is attracted to a fixed point O by a force kx, where k is a constant and x is the distance from O. The body is displaced from O and released from rest. Show that its subsequent motion is simple harmonic.

The table is now tilted at an angle α to the horizontal. Show that, if the oscillations of the body are along the line of maximum gradient through O, the motion is still simple harmonic. Find its new centre of oscillation relative to O.

The table is now made rough, with equal coefficients of static and dynamic friction, which cause a retarding force of μmg. Describe possible motions of the body when it is released from rest higher up the slope than O on the line of maximum gradient through O.

W8* Two unequal masses m_1 and m_2, joined by a light spring, rest on a smooth horizontal surface. The masses are pulled a small distance apart and then released. Show that the period T of the resulting oscillation is given by

$$T = 2\pi \left(\frac{m_1 m_2}{\mu(m_1 + m_2)} \right)^{1/2}$$

if a force μ, applied to the spring, causes unit extension.

A molecule of hydrogen chloride, HCl, vibrates at a frequency of 8.7×10^{13} Hz. How does the force per unit displacement between the hydrogen atom and the chlorine atom compare with that produced by a light spring, which, suspended vertically, extends by 1.0 cm when a mass of 0.50 kg is attached to its lower end?

[Relative atomic mass, A_r, of hydrogen is 1.0 and that of the more abundant naturally occurring isotope of chlorine is 35.]

W9 In the simple 'light pipe' shown in Fig. W9.1, a ray of light may be transmitted (with little loss) along the core by repeated total internal reflection at X, X', etc. The diagram shows a cross-section through a diameter of the 'pipe' with a ray incident in that plane.

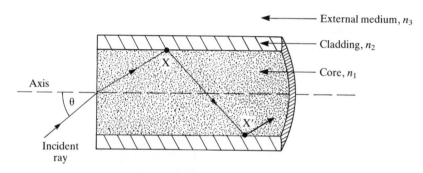

Fig. W9.1

The core, cladding and external medium have refractive indices n_1, n_2 and n_3, respectively. Show that the pipe will operate in this manner provided that the angle θ between the incident ray and the axis is smaller than a value θ_m, given by the expression

$$\sin \theta_m = \frac{(n_1^2 - n_2^2)^{1/2}}{n_3}.$$

Explain why the pipe does not work for rays for which $\theta > \theta_m$, and suggest why a cladding material is necessary in practice.

W10 Starting from first principles, derive the dimensions of a Young's double-slit arrangement that, using light of wavelength 589 nm, will produce dark fringes 0.02° apart on a distant screen.

What will be the angular fringe separation if the entire apparatus is immersed in a liquid of refractive index 1.33?

W11 White light from a vertical line source falls on two narrow vertical slits, 1.5 mm apart, and forms fringes on a screen 1 m away. Draw a carefully labelled diagram showing what is seen on the screen.

If a narrow vertical slit is located in the screen 2 mm from the central fringe, which wavelengths in the visible spectrum will *not* be present in the light transmitted through this slit?

W12 An opaque screen containing two narrow vertical slits, 0.5 mm apart, is placed on the table of a spectrometer and illuminated with a parallel beam of monochromatic light of wavelength $\lambda = 600$ nm. One slit transmits four times as much energy as the other. A lens of focal length 200 mm forms an image of the interference pattern on a screen placed in its focal plane. Describe, with the aid of a fully labelled sketch, the pattern that would be recorded.

W13 (a) A monochromatic beam of light of wavelength λ is incident at an angle α to the normal to a screen containing two narrow parallel slits separated by a distance d, as shown in Fig. W13.1. The beam emerges from the slits at an angle β to the normal.

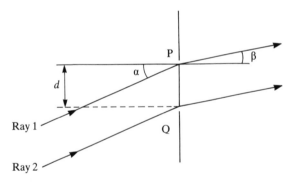

Fig. W13.1

Find an expression for the path difference between rays 1 and 2 in the emergent beam. Hence, find the condition for the light emerging at angle β to be of maximum intensity when brought to a focus.

(b) A parallel beam of X-rays of wavelength 1.4×10^{-10} m is incident on a line of identical atoms at an angle of 30° to the normal to the line. The atoms, which may be regarded as identical point scatterers of X-rays, are regularly spaced a distance 4.2×10^{-10} m apart. In which directions will X-rays be scattered strongly?

W14 In a Young's slits experiment, the primary slit S_0 is equidistant d from the twin slits S_1 and S_2, which are a distance y apart. All three slits are narrow and vertical. The slits S_1 and S_2 are a distance D from a white screen. If $y = 1.0 \times 10^{-3}\,\text{m}$, $d = 0.15\,\text{m}$ and $D = 1.0\,\text{m}$, calculate the positions of the five central bright fringes for
(a) blue light of wavelength 400 nm,
(b) red light of wavelength 650 nm.
Deduce from these calculations the nature of the pattern that would appear on the screen with white light.
*Slit S_0 is now moved horizontally a small distance δ parallel to the line joining the twin slits S_1 and S_2. By finding the new path difference to the slits $(S_0S_1 - S_0S_2)$, show that the fringe pattern moves a distance $D\delta/d$ in the opposite direction.
Hence deduce the effect of widening slit S_0 on the fringe pattern produced by monochromatic light. Estimate, for each of the wavelengths given above, any values for the width of S_0 that have particular significance.

W15 The diffraction grating in a simple spectrometer has 5×10^5 lines per metre. If the telescope of the spectrometer is replaced by a camera having a lens of focal length 0.4 m, what will be the separation in the second-order spectrum of the sodium D lines on the photographic plate?
[The wavelengths of the sodium D lines are 589.0 nm and 589.6 nm.]

W16 Light from a mercury lamp is incident normally on a diffraction grating ruled with 500 lines per millimetre. The spectrum contains two yellow lines, of wavelengths 577 nm and 579 nm. It is required to obtain an angular separation of these lines of at least $0.10°$. What orders of diffraction can be used?

W17 A parallel beam of monochromatic light falls onto a diffraction grating, making an angle θ with the normal to the grating. First-order spectra are found at angles of $11°$ and $53°$ to the normal and on opposite sides of the normal. Find the value of θ.
A second-order spectrum can be observed on one side of the normal but not on the other. Why is this so?

W18 (a) A diffraction grating having a spacing $d = 3.000\,\mu\text{m}$ is used in a spectrometer to investigate the emission spectrum of a mercury vapour discharge lamp. The spectrum is examined over the range of angles θ from $30°$ to $50°$, and maxima of intensity are observed at the angles and with the colours shown in the table. No other maxima are observed in this range of angles.

Violet	32.7°	42.4°
Blue	35.5°	46.6°
Green	33.1°	46.7°
Yellow	35.2°	35.4°

Use these data to calculate the wavelengths of the emission lines of the mercury vapour spectrum.

If the spectrum is now examined over all angles up to $\theta = 90°$, what will be the largest angle at which a maximum will be observed, and what colour will it be?

(b) Discuss the advantages and disadvantages of observing a spectrum at large values of θ.

W19 Two loudspeakers are mounted at ground level, 50 cm apart, and are connected in parallel to the output of an amplifier, which is fed from a variable-frequency oscillator. An observer, also at ground level, stands at a point that is 1.0 km from the line joining the loudspeakers and 1.0 km from the perpendicular bisector of that line. The oscillator is adjusted so that its frequency rises linearly with time, namely in such a way that at $t = 0$ the frequency is zero, at $t = 1.0$ s the frequency is 10 Hz, at $t = 2.0$ s the frequency is 20 Hz, and so on. The sound heard by the observer drops to a minimum for the first time at $t = 52.2$ s. Calculate the two possible values for the speed of sound.

W20 If the atmosphere is considered as a layer of air of uniform density equal to that of air at s.t.p. (standard temperature and pressure), calculate the thickness of such a layer.

Light from a star vertically overhead is cut off by the dark edge of the Moon's disc. Estimate the interval between the times of occultation as observed with red and blue light if the refractive indices of air at s.t.p. for these colours differ by 9.0×10^{-6}.

[Standard atmospheric pressure $= 1.01 \times 10^5$ Pa; density of air at s.t.p. $= 1.23$ kg m^{-3}.]

W21 Two microphones are placed near a source emitting sound at a wavelength of 45 mm. The microphones are respectively connected (via amplifiers) to the X and Y plates of an oscilloscope, and the trace on the screen is observed to be a straight line. On slowly changing the wavelength of the emitted sound, the same straight-line trace first reappears when the wavelength is 50 mm. What can be deduced concerning the distance of the microphones from the source?

One of the microphones is now moved with a constant speed directly away from the source, which is still emitting 50 mm wavelength sound waves. What appears to be a straight-line trace at the same orientation is seen at intervals of 10 s. What is the speed of the microphone and what is the apparent change in frequency detected by the moving microphone?

W22 A twin-engined light aircraft flies directly over a stationary observer on a still day. The engines are running at constant but slightly different speeds, so that the observer detects a low-frequency fluctuation in sound intensity. When the aircraft is approaching but is still very distant, the frequency of the fluctuation is 5.0 Hz. When it has receded to a great distance, the frequency is 3.0 Hz. Calculate the speed of the aircraft. What is the difference between the angular speeds of the engines, as measured by the pilot of the aircraft?

[Take the speed of sound in air to be $340 \, \mathrm{m \, s^{-1}}$.]

W23 Many police forces employ a speed detection device based on the Doppler effect using radar waves. The beam emitted by the device is reflected by the moving car and is detected at the radar unit: the difference in frequency between the emitted and reflected beams gives a measure of the speed of the car.

(a) Such a radar unit is mounted in a police car that is pursuing a stolen car along a straight road. At the instant when the speed of the police car is $30 \, \mathrm{m \, s^{-1}}$, the radar device records a fractional increase in the frequency of the reflected beam of 7.0×10^{-9}. What is the speed of the stolen car?

(b) It is more common for these devices to be operated from a stationary position rather than in a moving police car. Suggest why this is likely to lead to a more accurate determination of the speed of the suspect vehicle.

W24 If Δf is the change in frequency f, under what circumstances may the Doppler relationship

$$\Delta f / f = u / c$$

be applied, where u is the relative velocity of source and observer and c is the speed of the wave disturbance?

A spacecraft is in a circular orbit near the surface of the Moon in its equatorial plane. A radio transmitter at a tracking station on Earth radiates a frequency of 5.0 GHz. This radiation, received and amplified by the spacecraft, is retransmitted back to a receiver situated near the transmitter. A beat frequency is detected on Earth between the transmitted and received signals. When the Moon, observed from the tracking station, is high in the sky, the maximum beat frequency detected is 55 kHz, but at moonrise a maximum beat frequency of 64 kHz is measured. Assuming the Moon's orbit to be circular and the equators of Earth and Moon to be in the same plane, what can be deduced from these measurements?

[Speed of radio waves, $c = 3.0 \times 10^8 \,\mathrm{m\,s^{-1}}$; latitude of tracking station $= 52°\mathrm{N}$.]

W25* Show that the relation

$$c = (T/\mu)^{1/2}$$

connecting c, the speed of transverse waves on a wire, with T, the tension, and μ, the mass per unit length of the wire, is dimensionally correct.

A heavy chain of length l and mass per unit length μ is suspended from one end. A transverse wave is initiated at the uppermost end. Calculate the time taken by the wave to travel down and return to the top of the chain.

W26 A wire 1.0 m long, having a density of $8.0 \times 10^3 \,\mathrm{kg\,m^{-3}}$ and a radius of 0.10 mm, is kept taut by a tension of 1 N. The middle 5.0 cm lies in and at right angles to a uniform magnetic field that has a flux density of 0.5 T. What is the approximate deflection at the centre of the wire when a current of 1.0 A passes through the wire?

If an alternating current flows in the wire, at what frequencies will the deflection be greatest? Explain briefly how you would expect the electrical impedance of the wire to vary near these frequencies.

W27 The key on a piano corresponding to the note of frequency 880 Hz is depressed very gently, so that the hammer does not strike the string, but the damper is lifted and the string is free to vibrate. When the key corresponding to the note of frequency 440 Hz is struck firmly, it is found that the 880 Hz string also vibrates. Give a brief explanation of this phenomenon.

Suppose the 220 Hz string had also been free to vibrate. What frequencies, if any, would it have emitted when the 440 Hz key was struck?

W28 In a certain modulated wave that is being used for radio transmission, the electric field E varies with time t according to the expression

$$E = E_0(1 + m\sin 2\pi f_s t)\sin 2\pi f_c t,$$

where m is a measure of the degree of modulation and E_0 is a constant.

(a) If the wave form is represented by Fig. W28.1, determine the values of f_s and m.

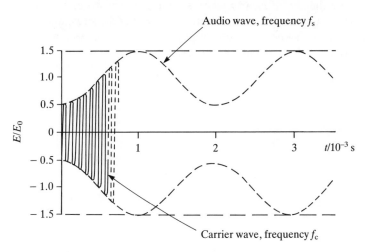

Fig. W28.1

(b) Show that the modulated wave form is equivalent to the linear superposition of three sinusoidal waves of frequencies $(f_c - f_s)$, f_c and $(f_c + f_s)$.

(c) Derive an expression for the ratio of the intensity of either side band (the waves of frequency $(f_c \pm f_s)$) to the intensity of the carrier wave, and draw a labelled graph of the frequency spectrum (i.e. a graph of intensity versus frequency) of the modulated wave form in Fig. W28.1.

(d) A certain radio station operating at a wavelength of 300 m is broadcasting a programme of music. Adequate quality is achieved at the receiver if audio frequencies up to a maximum of 10 kHz are reproduced. Calculate the range of frequencies present in the amplitude-modulated wave from this station.

Hence estimate the maximum number of radio stations that can transmit in the wavelength range 200 m to 600 m without interference between adjacent stations.

W29 Sound waves of frequency f and amplitude A are transmitted through a gas of density ρ. By considering each molecule of the gas to be undergoing simple harmonic motion, find D, the energy per unit volume due to the sound wave, in terms of f, A and ρ.

Hence show that the intensity I at a point in the path of the sound wave is given by $I = 2\pi^2 f^2 A^2 \rho v$, where v is the speed of the wave.

Problems

A point source of frequency 3.0 kHz radiates sound energy uniformly in air at the rate of 1.0 mW. At this frequency, an observer can hear the sound clearly when standing 150 m from the source. Assuming no absorption or reflection of the sound energy, and using approximate values of any quantities involved, estimate the amplitude of the wave at the observer.

Comment on your result.

Section SM

States of matter

SM1 A light horizontal wire is attached to two supports 1 m apart, so that it is just taut but has negligible tension. The diameter of the wire is 1.0 mm and the Young modulus for its material is 2×10^{11} Pa. A mass of 100 g is attached to the centre of the wire and allowed to fall. Calculate the distance through which it falls before beginning to rise again. Assume that this distance is small compared with the length of the wire.

SM2 A mass of 1.0 kg is firmly attached to a rigid beam by a copper wire and is supported so that the wire is vertical but unstretched. The support is removed. Show that, if Hooke's law is obeyed, only half the potential energy lost by the mass remains as elastic potential energy stored in the wire.

The mass is now raised to the level of the rigid beam and released. Find the minimum cross-sectional area of the wire if it is not to break. (Assume that the extension is always much less than the unstretched length of the wire and that Hooke's law is always obeyed.)

[For copper the Young modulus, $E = 1.1 \times 10^{11}$ Pa, and the tensile strength (maximum tensile stress), $\tau = 3.0 \times 10^{8}$ Pa.]

SM3 The greatest instantaneous acceleration a person can survive is $25g$, where g is the acceleration of free fall. A climber should therefore use a rope such that, if he or she falls when the rope is attached to a fixed point on a vertical rock, the fall will be survived.

A climber of mass m is attached to a rope that passes through a ring attached firmly to a rock face at B. The end of the rope is held by a companion, as shown in Fig. SM3.1. When the climber is at point A, a distance L above the ring, he falls; the companion holds the rope so that it binds at the ring at the instant the climber falls.

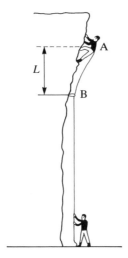

Fig. SM3.1

Assuming that the rope obeys Hooke's law up to breaking, use the principle of conservation of energy and the condition for greatest instantaneous acceleration to show that the part AB of the rope (of length L) must be able to stretch by more than $L/6$ without breaking for the climber to survive.

A particular rope has a breaking strength of 25 times the weight of a climber and obeys Hooke's law until breaking, when it has stretched by 20% of its length. Determine whether this rope is suitable.

SM4   As a stunt, a student plans to attach one end of a thick rubber rope to his waist and the other to the railing of a bridge. He will then jump off, free fall for a distance equal to the unstretched length of the rope and then be retarded by the rope as it stretches. He seeks your help, as a physicist, to calculate the length L of rope required to bring him to momentary rest just above the surface of the water beneath the bridge. The mass M of the student, the force constant k of the rope (the force required to produce unit extension) and the height H of the bridge above the water can all be measured. Air resistance and the mass of the rope can be neglected, and the rope can be assumed to obey Hooke's law.

(a) Find an expression for L, the length of the rope required, in terms of M, k, H and the acceleration of free fall, g.

(b) Draw a sketch graph to show how the velocity v of the student depends on time t throughout the motion, starting at the time he jumps off the bridge and continuing for two oscillations.

SM5 The Poisson ratio, σ, can be defined for a rod of circular cross-section under tension as the ratio of the lateral contraction per unit breadth to the longitudinal extension per unit length. Show that, for a wire that does not change in volume when stretched, $\sigma = 0.5$.

Comment on the following experimental values:

$$\sigma(\text{copper}) = 0.26; \quad \sigma(\text{iron}) = 0.27; \quad \sigma(\text{rubber}) = 0.48.$$

SM6 Give an account of an electrical method (not requiring the direct measurement of the lateral contraction) that you might use to determine the Poisson ratio (defined in question SM5) for a length of constantan wire of 0.193 mm diameter. You may assume that the resistivity of constantan does not change when strained. Give the theory of your method and an outline of the technique you would use in making any electrical measurements. Estimate the orders of magnitude of the quantities to be measured.

[The following approximate values for constantan may be useful: resistance of 0.193 mm diameter wire $= 20\,\Omega$ per metre; the Young modulus, $E = 2 \times 10^{11}$ Pa; and the Poisson ratio, $\sigma = 0.3$.]

SM7 A cable of mass m and area of cross-section A has length L when it is laid out on the ground and measured. It is then suspended vertically from one end.

(a) Draw a sketch graph showing how the stress σ in the cable depends on the distance x along it, measured from the point of suspension. Label the axes with appropriate values.

(b) By considering a small length δx of the suspended cable, show that the total energy stored as a result of the extension of the cable under its own weight is

$$Lm^2g^2/6AE,$$

where E is the Young modulus of the material of the cable. Assume that Hooke's law applies.

(c) The density ρ and the Young modulus E of a number of metals are tabulated below, the metals being listed in order of increasing density.

Metal	$\rho/\text{kg m}^{-3}$	E/Pa
aluminium	2.7×10^3	7.0×10^{10}
tin	7.3×10^3	5.0×10^{10}
copper	8.9×10^3	1.3×10^{11}
silver	1.1×10^4	8.3×10^{10}
tungsten	1.9×10^4	4.1×10^{11}

Suppose that cables of these materials, all of the same length and area of cross-section, hang vertically under their own weight. Write down a list of the metals in order of increasing strain energy. Show how you obtained this order.

SM8 The amount of heat required to convert 1 g of ice into vapour is approximately 3000 J. Estimate the energy required to separate one molecule from a single neighbour, assuming that, in ice, each H_2O molecule has four nearest neighbours.

[Relative molecular mass of water, $M_r = 18$.]

SM9 Sketch graphs showing how (a) the mutual potential energy U, (b) the interatomic force F, for the atoms of a diatomic molecule vary with the atomic separation x.

A simplified empirical formula for the mutual potential energy between the two atoms in a nitrogen molecule is

$$U = a/x^{12} - b/x^6,$$

where $a = 5 \times 10^{-138} \, J \, m^{12}$ and $b = 4 \times 10^{-78} \, J \, m^6$.

Find (i) the equilibrium separation x_0, (ii) the dissociation energy, (iii) the frequency of vibration about the equilibrium position.

[Mass of a nitrogen atom $= 2 \times 10^{-26}$ kg.]

SM10 A model of the carbon dioxide (CO_2) molecule is constructed as shown in Fig. SM10.1.

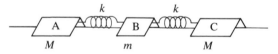

Fig. SM10.1

Two sliders A and C, each of mass M, represent the oxygen atoms and are connected by light springs, of force constant k, to a slider B of mass m, representing the carbon atom. All three sliders are placed on a linear air track (a device for ensuring almost frictionless motion). The two important modes of oscillation along the axis of the model molecule are as follows:

mode 1: B remains stationary, and A and C oscillate so that the centre of mass of the model molecule remains stationary;

mode 2: A and C move equal distances in one direction, and B moves in the opposite direction in such a way that the centre of mass again remains stationary.

(a) Find the frequency of oscillation in mode 1.

(b) Show that the frequency f_2 of mode 2 is given by

$$f_2 = (1/2\pi)[(k/M) + (2k/m)]^{1/2}.$$

(c) The absorption spectrum of carbon dioxide has a strong line at a wavelength of 3.9 μm associated with oscillations of the molecule in mode 2. At what other wavelength would you expect strong absorption?

[Relative atomic masses: oxygen, 16; carbon, 12.]

SM11* The singly ionised hydrogen molecule H_2^+ can be regarded as an electron of charge $-e$ moving in the field due to two protons, each of charge $+e$. The protons, which can be assumed to be stationary, are a distance r apart, as shown in Fig. SM11.1.

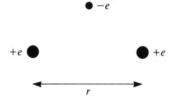

Fig. SM11.1

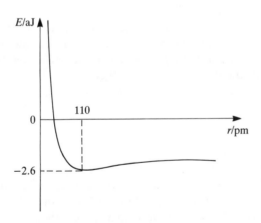

Fig. SM11.2

Fig. SM11.2 shows how the total electrostatic energy, E, of the ionised molecule in its state of lowest energy depends on the separation, r, of the protons. The zero of energy is the situation in which the electron and the protons are all infinitely far away from each other.

(a) The graph in Fig. SM11.2 can be considered as the summation of a positive energy term and a negative energy term. Identify the origins of these terms.

(b) What is the physical reason for the fact that, for small values of r, the graph has a large negative gradient?

(c) What is the physical interpretation of the fact that the curve shows a minimum energy at a particular value of r (110 pm)? [1 pm $= 1 \times 10^{-12}$ m.]

(d) What is the physical interpretation of the fact that the minimum value of the total energy is -2.6 aJ? [1 aJ $= 1 \times 10^{-18}$ J.]

(e) Calculate the contribution to the total energy at a proton–proton separation of 110 pm resulting from the presence of the electron.

(f) Suppose that the proton–proton separation is increased to a very large value. Where is the electron most likely to be found? Hence explain why, for large values of r, the curve tends towards a negative (non-zero) value of the total energy.

(g) The energy required to remove an electron from a hydrogen *atom* (the ionisation energy) is 2.2 aJ. Find the energy required to dissociate the singly ionised hydrogen *molecule* into a hydrogen atom and a proton at infinite separation. Explain your reasoning.

(h) If a second electron is added to the system of Fig. SM11.1, the neutral hydrogen molecule H_2 will be obtained. Explain qualitatively how you would expect the graph of the total electrostatic energy against proton separation for the neutral molecule to differ from that for the singly ionised molecule. Neglect the small contribution to the total energy caused by the mutual repulsion of the two electrons.

SM12 Sodium chloride crystallises in a cubic lattice with ions of sodium and chlorine arranged alternately at the corners of a cube, so that any ion has six nearest neighbours of the other element, as shown in Fig. SM12.1. X-ray measurements show that the distance, d, between the centres of adjacent sodium and chloride ions is 2.82×10^{-10} m. The relative atomic masses of sodium and chlorine are 23.0 and 35.5, respectively, and the density of sodium chloride is 2.17×10^3 kg m^{-3}. Use this information to deduce a value for the Avogadro constant.

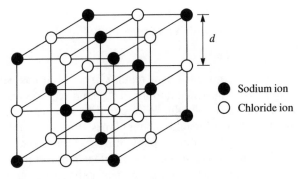

Fig. SM12.1

SM13 Fig. SM13.1 shows part of a crystal of sodium chloride, in which ions of sodium (charge $+e$) and chlorine (charge $-e$) are arranged alternately in a regular cubic lattice. The closest spacing between sodium and chloride ions is d. P is a chloride ion at the centre of this part of the crystal: its nearest neighbours are the six sodium ions in positions like ion A.

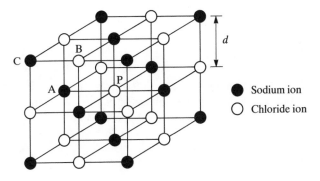

Fig. SM13.1

Draw up a table showing the numbers and distances from P of the sodium ions in positions similar to ion A, the chloride ions in positions similar to ion B and the sodium ions in positions similar to ion C. Hence find an expression in terms of the inter-ionic distance d for the electrostatic potential energy V_{es} of the chloride ion P due to all other ions in this part of the crystal.

The expression obtained for V_{es} approximates to the electrostatic potential energy of the ion P in the whole crystal. Given that the distance d in sodium chloride is 2.8×10^{-10} m, estimate the binding energy of one mole of sodium chloride.

SM14   Show that the strain energy U of a volume V of an elastic material obeying Hooke's law with Young modulus E under stress σ is

$$U = \sigma^2 V / 2E.$$

A solid may be modelled as a regular array of atoms with each atom bonded to Z near neighbours; each bond requires energy ε to break it. Breaking of a solid due to longitudinal stress can be assumed to be the separation of neighbouring planes of atoms of interplanar spacing x with surface planes containing n_s atoms per unit area. (You may assume that creating a new surface requires the breaking of half the bonds of each atom in the new surfaces.)

Suppose that a cylindrical rod of cross-sectional area A is broken to form two surfaces such that neighbouring planes of atoms are separated by the interatomic spacing x.

(a) Explain why an atom in the surface has greater energy than one in the bulk.

(b) Show that γ, the energy required to create unit area of surface, is given by

$$\gamma = n_s Z \varepsilon / 4.$$

(c) Using the expression derived for U, show that, if the solid obeys Hooke's law up until breaking, the breaking stress of the solid is given by

$$\sigma_{\max} = 2(E\gamma/x)^{1/2}.$$

Values of breaking stress calculated from this equation are from 10 to 1000 times greater than observed values. Account for this.

Section HK

Heat and kinetic theory

HK1 The bulb of a constant-volume gas thermometer has a volume V and is connected by a long narrow capillary tube to a manometer, where there is a dead space, of volume $V/4$, above the liquid. The thermometer is filled with an ideal gas at pressure p_0 and temperature T_0.

Find an expression for the sensitivity of the thermometer (rate of change of pressure with temperature) at temperature T if the manometer remains at temperature T_0.

Sketch the variation of sensitivity with temperature for the range $T/K = 0$ to ∞.

Show, on the same axes, sensitivity as a function of temperature for the same bulb connected to a manometer with dead space of negligible volume (a) when filled to give the same value of p_0 at T_0, (b) when filled with the same mass of gas as previously.

HK2 A constant-volume gas thermometer of volume $1 \times 10^{-3}\,\text{m}^3$ contains $0.05\,\text{mol}$ of a gas and is used to deduce values of temperature on the assumption that the ideal gas law is obeyed. In fact, *one mole* of the gas satisfies the relation

$$(p + a/V_{\text{m}}^2)(V_{\text{m}} - b) = RT,$$

where a corrects for intermolecular forces and b corrects for the effective size of the gas molecules.

(a) What form of the equation should be used for x moles of gas? Explain your answer.

(b) Given that the thermometer was calibrated at the triple point of water, use the data below to calculate the error when the thermometer is used to measure a temperature near that of boiling water:

$$a = 0.08\,\text{Pa}\,\text{m}^6\,\text{mol}^{-2}; \qquad b = 3 \times 10^{-5}\,\text{m}^3\,\text{mol}^{-1}.$$

HK3* Below 20 K, the specific heat capacity c of silver varies with temperature according to the equation

$$c/\mathrm{J\,kg^{-1}K^{-1}} = 1.5 \times 10^{-4}(T/K)^3 + 6.0 \times 10^{-3}T/\mathrm{K}.$$

If a small silver sphere of diameter 4 cm and at 20 K is placed in 25 g of liquid helium at 4 K, what fraction of the liquid will evaporate? [Density of silver $= 1.05 \times 10^4\,\mathrm{kg\,m^{-3}}$; specific latent heat of vaporisation of helium $= 2.1 \times 10^4\,\mathrm{J\,kg^{-1}}$; boiling point of helium $= 4\,\mathrm{K}$.]

HK4 At one possible site for the extraction of geothermal energy, the Earth's crust consists of a layer of shale 2.0 km thick above a layer of granite 4.0 km thick, as shown schematically in Fig. HK4.1.

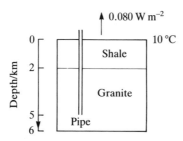

Fig. HK4.1

The surface temperature is 10 °C and the outward rate of flow of thermal energy at the surface is $0.080\,\mathrm{W\,m^{-2}}$. A pipe is to be sunk to a depth of 5.0 km. Calculate the expected temperature at the lower end of this pipe.

[Thermal conductivities: shale, $1.3\,\mathrm{W\,m^{-1}\,K^{-1}}$, granite, $3.5\,\mathrm{W\,m^{-1}\,K^{-1}}$.]

HK5 A pond of water at 0 °C is freezing. The thickness of the ice layer is h and the top surface of the ice remains at a temperature θ ($\theta < 0\,°\mathrm{C}$). Derive an equation for the rate of increase of h in terms of θ, l, h, λ and ρ, where l is the specific latent heat of fusion, λ is the thermal conductivity and ρ is the density of ice. Calculate the rate of increase when $h = 150\,\mathrm{mm}$ and $\theta = -4\,°\mathrm{C}$.

Discuss briefly how the rate of formation of ice would be affected if the temperature of the water in the pond was 0 °C at the water–ice interface but increased with depth to 4 °C at the bottom of the pond.

[Specific latent heat of fusion of ice, $l = 3.3 \times 10^5\,\mathrm{J\,kg^{-1}}$; thermal conductivity of ice, $\lambda = 2.3\,\mathrm{W\,m^{-1}\,K^{-1}}$; density of ice, $\rho = 920\,\mathrm{kg\,m^{-3}}$.]

HK6 A cubical oven of side 10 cm is insulated on all its faces by a layer of asbestos 2.0 mm thick; the outside of the asbestos is maintained at 20 °C. One junction of a copper–constantan thermocouple is mounted within the oven, the other being in the steam above water boiling at normal pressure. The leads from the thermocouple are connected to an amplifier of voltage gain 1.0×10^7. The output from the amplifier, which has negligible internal resistance, feeds a heater coil of resistance $10 \, \Omega$ within the oven. What is the temperature inside the oven when the system has reached a steady state? Assume that the inside of the oven is at a uniform temperature.

[Thermal conductivity of asbestos, $k = 1.5 \times 10^{-1} \, \text{W m}^{-1} \text{K}^{-1}$; thermo-e.m.f of copper–constantan $= 4.0 \times 10^{-5} \, \text{V K}^{-1}$.]

HK7 The ends of a uniform rod, 10 cm long, are maintained at temperatures of 4 K and 1 K. What is the temperature distribution along the rod if

(a) the thermal conductivity is constant and heat transfer through the sides of the rod is negligible,

(b) the thermal conductivity is constant but heat transfer through the sides of the rod is significant, the rod gaining heat from the surroundings,

(c) there is no heat transfer through the sides of the rod but the thermal conductivity is proportional to thermodynamic temperature?

Give quantitative answers where possible.

HK8 A long thin copper strip of width 5.0 mm is sandwiched between two sheets of asbestos 1.0 mm thick; the outside of the asbestos is maintained at 0 °C.

Show that, at a certain current, the temperature will increase indefinitely, and calculate this current. Assume that the flow of heat is normal to the strip.

[Resistance per unit length of the copper strip at a Celsius temperature θ is given by

$$R_1 = a(1 + b\theta),$$

where $a = 2.2 \times 10^{-2} \, \Omega \, \text{m}^{-1}$ and $b = 4.3 \times 10^{-3} \, \text{K}^{-1}$; thermal conductivity of asbestos, $k = 1.3 \times 10^{-1} \, \text{W m}^{-1} \text{K}^{-1}$.]

HK9* The thermal conductivity of a gas at a thermodynamic temperature T is proportional to $T^{1/2}$. Two vessels, containing gas maintained at temperatures θ of 100 °C and 0 °C respectively, are joined by a perfectly lagged glass tube. If convection effects in the gas and heat conducted by the tube may be ignored, show that the temperature of the gas at the midpoint of the tube when a steady state is reached is 52.0 °C.

HK10* A metallic rod of length L and cross-sectional area A carries a current I. What is the rate of generation of heat per unit length if the electrical resistance between its ends is R?

If the rod, having thermal conductivity λ, is thermally insulated so that the only loss of heat occurs at its two ends (which remain at a temperature θ), derive an expression for the temperature gradient along the rod at a distance l from its midpoint. Hence, or otherwise, find the temperature at the midpoint, using the values given below.

What fundamental difficulties are there in using this method to measure thermal conductivities?

$[I = 25.0\,\text{A}; A = 12.5\,\text{mm}^2; L = 0.10\,\text{m}; \lambda = 3.85 \times 10^2\,\text{W m}^{-1}\,\text{K}^{-1};$ $R = 1.25 \times 10^{-3}\,\Omega; \theta = 20.0\,^\circ\text{C.}]$

HK11 Derive an expression connecting the pressure of a gas with its density and the mean-square speed of its molecules. Show that this expression is consistent with the equation of state of an ideal gas provided a certain assumption is made.

Find the total kinetic energy per unit volume in a monatomic gas at standard temperature and pressure and deduce an expression for the variation of this kinetic energy with temperature if the pressure is maintained constant.

[Standard pressure $= 1.01 \times 10^5\,\text{Pa.}$]

HK12 In a low-pressure mercury discharge tube, the vapour is effectively at 1000 K. What is the root-mean-square speed of the atoms?

If the lamp emits a green line at 546 nm, estimate the spread in wavelength due to the motion of the atoms.

Why is the intensity of the line greatest at the centre?

[Assume that mercury vapour behaves as an ideal monatomic gas of relative atomic mass 200.]

HK13* Derive an expression for the number of impacts of gas molecules on unit area in unit time in terms of the number of molecules per unit volume, n, and their mean speed, $\langle c \rangle$. Explain the assumptions you make.

A disc of radius a rotates with constant angular velocity ω in a gas at low pressure so that the molecules of the gas strike the disc from random directions. If the molecules are momentarily attached to the disc and leave in random directions relative to the disc, derive an expression for the torque exerted on the disc by the gas in terms of $\langle c \rangle$, the mean speed of the gas molecules, ρ, the density of the gas, a and ω.

HK14 The residual gas in a vacuum chamber of volume $5.0 \times 10^{-3} \, \text{m}^3$ is oxygen at a pressure of $1.0 \times 10^{-7} \, \text{Pa}$, at room temperature. An experiment on the surface electronic properties of silicon is carried out in this vacuum chamber. A clean surface may be exposed when desired by cleaving the semiconductor mechanically but its properties are significantly modified if the ratio of adsorbed oxygen molecules to semiconductor atoms on the surface exceeds 1 in 100. The semiconductor sample has a surface area of $8 \times 10^{-5} \, \text{m}^2$ and there are about 2×10^{15} semiconductor atoms in the surface layer. Each oxygen molecule incident on the silicon surface may be assumed to adhere to it and, because of leaks from the exterior, the pressure of oxygen in the chamber remains constant at $1.0 \times 10^{-7} \, \text{Pa}$. Estimate the time available for observations on the clean surface before its properties are significantly affected by adsorbed oxygen.

[Relative molecular mass of oxygen = 32.]

HK15 A square frame of side 10 cm rests on a table. Confined within the frame are 500 ants, each of mass $1.0 \times 10^{-3} \, \text{g}$. The ants rush about randomly with constant speed $2.0 \times 10^{-2} \, \text{m s}^{-1}$, colliding with each other and with the walls. Assuming the collisions are perfectly elastic, calculate the force on each side of the square due to the ants' movement.

HK16 A stream of particles, each of mass m and having kinetic energy E, is collimated into a parallel beam of cross-sectional area A. The particles are incident normally on a smooth plane surface at rate n and they rebound elastically. Derive an expression for the pressure on the surface in terms of A, m, E and n. At the appropriate places in the derivation, give clear statements of any of Newton's laws of motion that may be involved.

Explain why the pressure would be different if the surface were rough so that the particles rebounded at various angles.

An electric light bulb emits 20 W of radiation uniformly in all directions. What is the maximum radiation pressure on a surface placed 2.0 m away from the bulb? State the conditions under which this will occur.

HK17 A feature of the quantum behaviour of light is that photons of energy hf have momentum hf/c, so that when light is reflected or absorbed by a surface a pressure is exerted on that surface. An evacuated cubical box of side a is constructed with perfectly reflecting interior surfaces; initially, it is dark inside. A small window is opened to allow light of frequency f to enter the container and is also closed again when the box contains N photons.

(a) Assuming that the photons behave like the molecules of an ideal gas, use simple kinetic theory ideas to show that the pressure inside the box when equilibrium is established is $Nhf/3a^3$.

(b) For a box of side 0.50 m, how many photons of light of wavelength 630 nm are required to create a pressure equal to atmospheric $(1.0 \times 10^5 \text{ Pa})$?

Consider now a box of the same dimensions containing not photons, but an ideal gas at room temperature and atmospheric pressure.

(c) Estimate the number of molecules in the box.

(d) When the volume of the box containing the gas is suddenly decreased, both pressure and temperature increase. Why is this?

(e) Suggest what might happen if the volume of the box containing the *photons* were suddenly reduced.

HK18 A vessel is divided into two parts of equal volume by a partition in which there is a very small hole. Initially, each part contains gas at 300 K and a low pressure, p. One part of the vessel is now heated to 600 K while the other is maintained at 300 K. If a steady state is established when the rate at which molecules pass through the hole from each side is the same, find the resulting pressure difference between the two parts.

HK19 Explain the application of the principle of conservation of energy to thermal systems.

Two cylinders A and B of equal volume V contain the same ideal gas at temperature T and at pressures $2p$ and p respectively. A valve connecting the two cylinders is opened slightly and, as the gas leaks from A to B, the pressure in A is maintained at $2p$ by pushing in a piston. The process is continued until the gas in cylinder B is also at $2p$. If there is good thermal contact between the cylinders but they are thermally insulated from their surroundings, find

(*a*) the final temperature in terms of T,

(*b*) the final volume of gas in cylinder A in terms of V.

[Molar heat capacity of the gas at constant volume, $C_{V,m} = 3R/2$.]

HK20 (a) Bromine gas at atmospheric pressure and room temperature has a density of 6.4 kg m^{-3}. Given that the atmospheric pressure is approximately $1.0 \times 10^5 \text{ Pa}$, find the approximate r.m.s. speed of bromine molecules.

Experiments show that bromine molecules take about 500 s to diffuse 0.1 m in air. This low speed compared with the r.m.s. speed can be attributed to the random collisions of bromine and air molecules. A bromine molecule travels an average distance λ between successive collisions and makes n collisions in travelling from A to B (Fig. HK20.1). The distance x is given by $x = \lambda\sqrt{n}$.

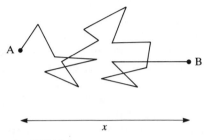

Fig. HK20.1

(b) Assuming that the bromine molecules are moving at their r.m.s. speed over this random path, estimate the number of collisions suffered by a molecule in diffusing 0.1 m. Show that λ, the mean free path, is approximately 1×10^{-7} m.

(c) By considering the motion of one bromine molecule through the air molecules, show that one bromine molecule will effectively occupy, on average, a volume of $\pi d^2 \lambda$, where d is the diameter of a bromine molecule. (Assume the air molecules to be stationary and to have the same size as bromine molecules.)

(d) Given that a volume of bromine liquid will expand approximately 500 times when it becomes a gas, estimate the diameter of a bromine molecule.

(e) It is known that the air molecules would move with an r.m.s. speed of approximately $500 \, \text{m s}^{-1}$, that air molecules are smaller than bromine molecules and that each bromine molecule consists of two bromine atoms. Discuss whether these facts have any significant effects on your estimates of λ and d.

HK21 (a) A gas molecule of mass m is subjected to a constant external force F. By writing down two equations for the momentum change between collisions, find an expression for its mean drift velocity v, in terms of m, F and τ, the mean time between collisions with other molecules.

(b) In unit volume of a certain gas, there are n molecules, of which n^* are singly ionized ($n^* \ll n$). Find an expression for the electrical conductivity of the gas in terms of n^*, e, τ and m, where e is the electronic charge.

(c) Given that the mean distance between collisions is $0.23/(nS^2)$, where S is the molecular diameter, obtain an expression for τ in terms of m, n, S, T (the temperature) and the Boltzmann constant k.

(d) Hence estimate the electrical conductivity of nitrogen at 300 K, if the fraction of molecules that are singly ionized is 1 in 10^6.

[Relative molecular mass of nitrogen $= 28$ and its molecular diameter $= 0.3$ nm.]

HK22 At an altitude of about 100 km above the Earth's surface, the density and temperature of the atmosphere are about 1.0×10^{-14} kg m^{-3} and 2000 K, respectively. At this altitude, the major constituent of the atmosphere is atomic oxygen. Use this information to estimate the pressure of the atmosphere at an altitude of 1000 km. On average, how far apart are the oxygen atoms? What is their root-mean-square speed? Discuss whether the temperature of a gas at this pressure can be interpreted in the same way as the temperature of a gas at normal atmospheric pressure.

[Relative atomic mass of oxygen $= 16$.]

HK23 One cubic decimetre of an ideal gas at atmospheric pressure is expanded isothermally until its volume is doubled. It is then compressed to its original volume at constant pressure. Finally, it is compressed isothermally to its original pressure.

Show these processes on a p–V diagram and calculate the total work done on the gas.

If 126 J of heat were removed from the gas during the second stage at constant pressure, what was the total change in the internal energy between the initial and final states?

HK24 The simplified p–V diagram for the steam chamber of an early steam engine is shown in Fig. HK24.1.

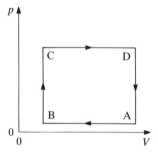

Fig. HK24.1

Identify the physical processes involved in the cycle ABCD.

The engine had a cylindrical chamber of diameter 0.54 m and length 2.4 m, and made a complete cycle every 5.0 s. Given that the steam entered the chamber at atmospheric pressure (1.0×10^5 Pa), determine the theoretical output power of the engine.

If, in fact, the engine was only able to lift 46 kg of water through 46 m at each cycle, what was the actual output power, expressed as a percentage of the theoretical output power?

HK25 A perfectly smooth cylindrical piston of mass m and cross-sectional area A fits closely into a horizontal tube sealed at both ends with flat plates. In the position of equilibrium, the length of the air column on each side of the piston is l and the air pressure is p. Show that, if the piston is disturbed slightly, it will subsequently move with simple harmonic motion, and determine the length of the equivalent simple pendulum. (Assume that the motion takes place under isothermal conditions.)

HK26* When unit mass of liquid at its boiling point is converted into vapour at the same temperature, an input of thermal energy (the specific latent heat of vaporisation) is required. State how, if at all, the internal energy changes during this change of state at constant temperature. Is mechanical work done on or by the system? Explain your answers.

Unit mass of water at 20 °C is completely converted into water vapour at the same temperature by two different methods:

    (a)   water at 20 °C → water vapour at 20 °C;

    (b)   (i) water at 20 °C → water at 100 °C;

          (ii) water at 100 °C → water vapour (steam) at 100 °C;

          (iii) water vapour at 100 °C → water vapour at 20 °C.

In each method, atmospheric pressure remains constant at 1.0×10^5 Pa.

Explain how any change of internal energy in method (a) is related to the net change of internal energy in method (b).

Explain how any mechanical work done on or by the system in method (a) is related to the net mechanical work in method (b).

Explain how the thermal energy (heat) input to the system in method (a) is related to the net thermal energy input in method (b).

Hence deduce the specific latent heat of vaporisation of water at 20 °C from the following data.

Specific heat capacity of water between 20 °C and 100 °C $= 4.2 \times 10^3 \, \text{J kg}^{-1} \text{K}^{-1}$.

Specific heat capacity of water vapour between 20 °C and 100 °C (measured at constant pressure) $= 2.0 \times 10^3 \, \text{J kg}^{-1} \text{K}^{-1}$.

Specific latent heat of vaporisation of water at 100 °C and 1.0×10^5 Pa $= 2.26 \times 10^6 \, \text{J kg}^{-1}$.

Explain why your answer is not simply $2.26 \times 10^6 \, \text{J kg}^{-1}$.

Section ES

Electrostatics

ES1 Explain how (a) the potential, (b) the electric field, at a point due to a number of point charges can be obtained by summing the effects of the individual charges.

Equal and opposite charges $+Q$ and $-Q$ are a distance $2a$ apart. Taking the midpoint between them as the origin O, find the potential and the field at a point P that is a distance r ($\gg a$) from O when

(c) P is on the line joining the charges,

(d) P is on a perpendicular bisector of the line joining the charges.

Equal and opposite charges separated by a small distance constitute a dipole. A hydrogen chloride molecule may be treated as a dipole in which an electron is separated from an equal positive charge by 2×10^{-11} m. Calculate the work required to turn a hydrogen chloride molecule that is lying parallel to a field of 3×10^5 V m^{-1} through $180°$.

Suggest an explanation for the fact that the number of hydrogen chloride molecules lying nearly parallel to an applied field increases if the temperature is reduced.

ES2* In a simplified form of the Rutherford model of the atom, the positive charge Q can be assumed to be *uniformly distributed* throughout a sphere of radius a, corresponding to the nucleus. Show that the electric field has a maximum value at the surface of the sphere and that it decreases linearly with radius from the surface to zero at the centre.

Find also the variation of electrostatic potential with distance from the centre of the sphere for radii both less than and greater than a.

Discuss qualitatively how the electrostatic potential outside the nucleus will vary with the radius if the nucleus is surrounded by the electrons of the neutral atom.

ES3 Two powdered minerals in a mixture become oppositely charged when placed in a vibrating tray. This charging by friction forms the basis of a mineral separation method. One side of the tray is open and immediately after leaving the tray the minerals fall vertically between electrodes maintaining a uniform horizontal field of $1.0 \times 10^3 \, V \, m^{-1}$. Given that the specific charge acquired by the minerals is $\pm 4.0 \times 10^{-6} \, C \, kg^{-1}$, through what vertical distance must the minerals fall to achieve a 10 cm separation?

What assumptions have been made in your calculation?

ES4 When a point charge q is placed at P a distance a above an infinite horizontal earthed conducting sheet, the distribution of electric fields in space is similar to that obtained if the conducting sheet is replaced by a charge $-q$ placed at P′, which is a distance $2a$ vertically below P.

What is the force between the charge q and the conducting sheet?

If R is a point on the surface of the conducting sheet at a distance x from the line PP′, find

(a) the electric field intensity just above R,

(b) the surface density of charge at R.

Two very large earthed plane conducting sheets meet at an angle of 90°. A particle of mass m carrying a charge q lies on the plane bisecting this angle. Initially, the particle is held at rest at a distance a from the line on which the sheets intersect. Using the concept of image charges, find expressions for

(c) the force on the particle,

(d) the speed at which it strikes the conductors when released.

ES5 A long straight wire in free space carries a uniform distribution of positive charge of σ per unit length. Without disturbing the charge distribution, the wire (of radius r) is surrounded by a solid insulator of internal and external radii r and R respectively, made of material of relative permittivity ε_r. Sketch a graph, labelled with appropriate values, showing how the electric field E varies with distance x from the axis of the wire, for values of x from r to $2R$. Use your graph to find the electric potential difference V between the wire and the outer surface of the insulator.

ES6 A conducting wire bent into a circular loop of radius R carries a total positive charge Q. P is a point on the axis of the loop, distance x from its centre O (Fig. ES6.1). S is an element of the wire, small enough for the charge on it to be considered as a point charge δQ.

(a) Give the magnitude and direction of the electric field strength at P due to the point charge δQ at S.

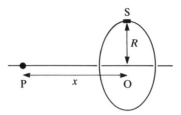

Fig. ES6.1

(b) Hence find the magnitude and direction of the field strength E at P due to the total charge on the loop. Why would you expect this field strength to have a maximum value when P is at a point on the axis a finite distance from O? (This finite distance, which you are *not* expected to derive, is $R/\sqrt{2}$.)

(c) Write down the electric potential V at P due to the total charge Q. For what position of P is the potential a maximum? Sketch a graph showing how V varies with x.

An electron of charge $-e$ and mass m_e is released from rest on the axis of the loop at a distance $R/\sqrt{2}$ from the plane of the loop.

(d) Sketch a graph showing how the potential energy V_p of the electron varies with distance x from the plane of the loop.

(e) The electron passes through the loop with speed v. Show that v is given by

$$v^2 = eQ[1 - (2/3)^{1/2}]/2\pi\varepsilon_0 m_e R,$$

where ε_0 is the permittivity of free space.

Describe qualitatively the subsequent motion of the electron, making reference to your graph of V_ρ against x.

ES7* (a) A disc of radius r carries a charge q uniformly distributed *around its rim*. Find expressions for the electric potential and electric field strength at a point P which is on the axis of the disc and at a distance x from the centre.

(b) Hence show that, for a charge q, uniformly distributed *over the whole disc*, the electric potential at P is given by

$$V = q[(r^2 + x^2)^{1/2} - x]/2\pi r^2\varepsilon_0.$$

(c) Determine the corresponding value for the electric field E. Does the value of E reduce to the expected results if (i) $x \gg r$, (ii) $x \ll r$?

ES8* The diagram (Fig. ES8.1) shows a simple torsion balance. This works on the principle that, when the rod is twisted in the horizontal plane, the couple produced in the torsion wire is equal to a constant times

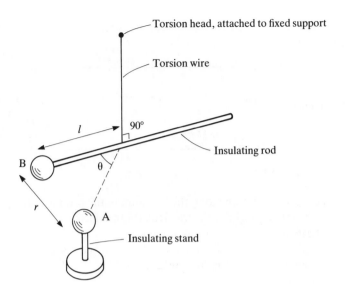

Fig. ES8.1

the angle of twist. An additional couple can be applied to the insulating rod by twisting the torsion head.

A small conducting sphere A is mounted on a fixed insulating stand and an identical small conducting sphere B is attached to the horizontal insulating rod. When A and B are uncharged, they are touching and the torsion wire is untwisted. When A and B are given the same positive charge, the spheres separate and the rod comes to rest at an angular deflection θ of 0.25 rad. The torsion head is now rotated through 0.5 rad in the same sense as the initial deflection of the rod and the charge on B is replaced by one of equal magnitude but opposite sign. Show that the system is now in equilibrium when the rod is at an angle of about 0.4 rad to its original position.

By considering a small displacement from this position, show that the equilibrium is stable. Also discuss whether there is any other equilibrium position.

[The approximation $r \approx l\theta$ may be used throughout.]

ES9 An ionisation chamber consists of two parallel plates of area A a distance d apart separated by air and carrying charges $\pm Q$. A burst of ionising radiation passes through the chamber, producing a thin layer of ionised air. This layer is parallel to the plates, is initially midway between them and occupies the entire area of the capacitor. The free charges in the ionised layer amount to $\pm fQ$, where $f < 1$. The sheet of positive and negative ions separate at a constant rate, the distance between them at a certain time being x, as shown in Fig. ES9.1.

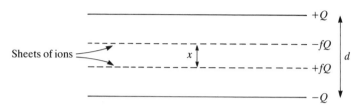

Fig. ES9.1

Sketch the variation along the line joining the centres of the plates of (a) the intensity of the electric field, (b) the electric potential, when the sheets are in the positions shown.

Calculate the potential difference between the plates in terms of d, Q, f, x and ε_0. What is the capacitance C of the chamber?

Describe how V and C change as x increases.

ES10 The plates of a parallel-plate capacitor of area $10^{-2}\,\text{m}^2$ are separated by a distance of 10 mm. A layer of dielectric 3.0 mm thick of relative permittivity 6.0 lies between the plates and is adjacent to one plate. What is the capacitance of the capacitor if the remaining space is air?

If a 100 V battery is connected across the capacitor with the negative terminal earthed and connected to the plate adjacent to the dielectric, what is the potential at the interface between the dielectric and the air?

A very thin sheet of material also of area $10^{-2}\,\text{m}^2$ carrying a uniformly distributed positive charge of surface density $5.0 \times 10^{-7}\,\text{C m}^{-2}$ is inserted at the interface and covers the dielectric. What is the potential of the sheet if the battery remains connected?

ES11 For every dielectric material there is a greatest value E_0 of the electric field that the material will withstand; above this value, the insulation breaks down. Using this information, show that the greatest energy that can be stored in a parallel-plate capacitor with a given dielectric material is dependent only on the volume of the dielectric. Find an expression for the greatest energy per unit volume of dielectric in terms of E_0 and other constants.

ES12 Derive an expression for the energy stored in a charged capacitor.

A parallel-plate capacitor consists of square plates arranged vertically, separated by 5.0 mm of air, with the upper edges horizontal. The capacitor is charged by momentarily connecting it to a 1000 V battery and is then lowered so that the bottom edges touch the surface of an insulating liquid of relative permittivity 80.

Determine how high the liquid will rise between the plates if it has a density of $10^3 \, \text{kg m}^{-3}$. (Neglect surface tension and viscosity effects.)

ES13 A capacitor is constructed from two large square plates of side a, a distance d $(\ll a)$ apart. A large rectangular sheet of insulating material, thickness d and relative permittivity ε_r is inserted between the plates a distance x $(< a)$ measured from one edge of the capacitor plates. Making use of Gauss' law and the definition of capacitance, show that the capacitance of the system is

$$\varepsilon_0 a[a + (\varepsilon_r - 1)x]/d.$$

The capacitor is charged to a potential difference of $100 \, \text{V}$ and then connected to a resistance of $10^{10} \, \Omega$. If the area of the plates is $0.25 \, \text{m}^2$, the plate separation is $2 \, \text{mm}$ and $\varepsilon_r = 3.0$, at what speed and in which direction must the insulating sheet be moved to keep the potential difference between the capacitor plates constant?

Show that, if the capacitor also loses charge because the insulating sheet has an appreciable conductivity σ, it is not possible to keep the potential difference constant by moving the insulating sheet at constant speed.

ES14 A capacitor consists of two parallel plates of area A mounted a distance x apart in a liquid of relative permittivity ε_r. The capacitor is isolated and carries a charge Q. Calculate from first principles, proving any formulae you use,

(a) the energy W stored in the capacitor,

(b) the change of W if the separation between the plates is increased by a small amount Δx,

(c) hence, or otherwise, the force per unit area on each plate of the capacitor as a function of E, the electric field between the plates,

(d) the work done against electrical forces in removing all the liquid from the space between the plates.

ES15* Starting from first principles, show that the capacitance of an isolated spherical conductor of radius a is $4\pi\varepsilon_0 a$.

The electrical energy stored when an isolated conductor is charged can be thought of as residing in the electric field E associated with the charge distribution on the conductor. Show that the value given above for the capacitance of an isolated sphere is consistent with a field energy of $\varepsilon_0 E^2/2$ per unit volume summed over all space.

ES16 Define the *relative permittivity* ε_r of a dielectric.

The parallel plates of a capacitor carry charges $\pm Q$ and the narrow space between them is filled with dielectric of relative permittivity ε_r.

If charges $\mp Q'$ are induced on the dielectric adjacent to each plate, show that $\varepsilon_r = Q/(Q - Q')$.

An experiment to measure the relative permittivity of water employs a parallel-plate capacitor, which is immersed in the water. The plates are square and of side 0.10 m and their separation d is variable. The capacitor is charged up to 300 V, using a d.c. supply, and is then discharged through a coulomb meter. The series of values obtained for charge Q on the capacitor as a function of d is given below.

d/m	0.020	0.040	0.060	0.080	0.100
Q/nC	106	56	41	35	32

Calculate a value for ε_r.

ES17* An air-spaced capacitor, which is initially uncharged and of capacitance C, is connected in series with a resistor of high resistance R and a battery of negligible internal resistance and e.m.f. V. Deduce separately and from first principles (a) the energy lost by the battery, (b) the energy gained by the capacitor, (c) the energy dissipated in the resistor. Show that your results are consistent with energy conservation.

Oil of relative permittivity 3 now flows into the capacitor. Discuss the energy changes that occur in each component of the system if the oil flows in (i) very slowly, (ii) very quickly.

Section E

Current electricity

E1 The temperature coefficients of resistance of certain alloys are positive whereas others are negative. This makes it possible to combine wires of different alloys to construct a resistor that has a resistance that does not vary with temperature. Wires of constantan and manganin are available having resistances per unit length r (measured at $0\,°C$) given in the table below. The temperature coefficients of resistance α are also listed.

Wire	$r/\Omega\,m^{-1}$	$\alpha/(°C)^{-1}$
constantan	6.3	-3.0×10^{-5}
manganin	5.3	$+1.4 \times 10^{-5}$

What lengths L_c and L_m of the constantan and manganin wires should be connected in series to form a resistor of constant resistance $5.0\,\Omega$?

E2 (a) A copper wire and an aluminium wire of the same length have the same potential difference applied to them. Show that it is impossible to choose radii that will make the current density the same in each wire.

(b) Two such wires of equal diameter are arranged parallel and vertical and their ends are joined to form a thermoelectric circuit with one junction at the top and the other at the bottom. If the rate of change of temperature with height is constant and if the thermoelectric e.m.f. is proportional to temperature difference, show that the electric power dissipated in the wires is proportional to the volume of the wires.

E3 A certain galvanometer has a resistance, r, of $500\,\Omega$ and gives a full-scale deflection for a current of $200\,\mu$A. This meter is connected as shown in Fig. E3.1 to make a multi-range current meter.

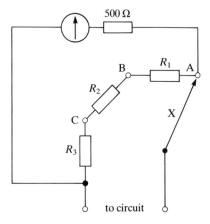

Fig. E3.1

Connection to the circuit is made at the terminals shown. The currents in the external circuit needed to give full-scale deflections when X is connected to A, B and C in turn are shown in the table.

X connected to	Current /mA
A	1
B	10
C	100

Find the values of the resistors R_1, R_2 and R_3.

E4 State the laws that are used to determine the flow of current in a network of resistors.

A known resistance R ($1200\,\Omega$) and an unknown resistance R_x are connected in series with a cell of negligible internal resistance. When a certain voltmeter of internal resistance r is connected across R, it reads 0.6 V, and when it is connected across R_x, it reads 0.9 V. Find the resistance R_x.

When the voltmeter is connected *in series* with R and R_x, it reads 0.8 V. What can you deduce about the cell and the voltmeter?

E5 A simple form of underfloor heating for a room 6 m long and 5.5 m wide consists of an array of wire netting through which current may be passed. Part of the array is shown in Fig. E5.1. All the holes in

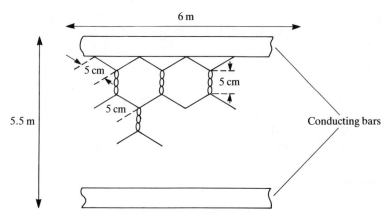

Fig. E5.1

the netting are regular hexagons of side 5 cm. One pair of opposite sides of each hexagon lies parallel to the shorter side of the room and consists of double strands of wire twisted together; all other edges consist of single strands. At each of the longer sides of the room, the whole width of the netting is connected to a conducting bar.

If the supply voltage is 240 V r.m.s., what diameter of wire should be used to dissipate approximately 3 kW as heat within the room? (Neglect edge effects.)

[Resistivity of material of wire $= 1.1 \times 10^{-6}\,\Omega\,\text{m}$.]

E6 The current I through a rod of a certain metallic oxide is given by $I/\text{A} = 0.20\,(V/\text{V})^3$, where V is the potential difference across it. The rod is connected in series with a resistance to a 6.0 V battery of negligible internal resistance. What values should the series resistance have so that (a) the current in the circuit is 0.40 A, (b) the power dissipated in the rod is twice that dissipated in the resistance?

E7* In a certain cathode-ray tube, the current is 10 μA and the electrons strike the screen uniformly over a circular spot of diameter 2 mm in the centre of the screen, which has a diameter of 20 cm. The screen is coated with a film of aluminium 1 μm thick. This prevents accumulation of charge, which flows away radially to an electrode surrounding the screen. Calculate the resistance and hence the potential difference between the edge of the spot and the edge of the screen.

Would you expect this potential difference to affect the spot on the screen?

[Resistivity of aluminium $= 2.8 \times 10^{-8}\,\Omega\,\text{m}$.]

E8* A metal hemisphere of radius 0.1 m is immersed near the centre of a large conducting tank containing a liquid of resistivity $60\,\Omega\,\text{m}$. The plane surface of the hemisphere is level with the surface of the liquid.

Find an expression for the resistance between two hemispherical shells within the liquid, concentric with the centre of the metal hemisphere, having radii r and $(r + \delta r)$ respectively. Hence, calculate the resistance between the hemisphere and the tank.

When a potential difference of 1000 V is applied between the hemisphere and the tank, where will the initial rate of rise of temperature be greatest? Estimate its value if $1.70 \times 10^6\,\text{J}$ are required to raise the temperature of $1.0\,\text{m}^3$ of the liquid by 1.0 K.

E9 (a) A power line in the national grid, operated at 132 kV r.m.s and supplying 55 MW of input power, consists of a core of seven steel strands, each 0.28 cm in diameter, surrounded by 30 aluminium strands of the same diameter. The relevant tensile and electrical properties of steel and aluminium are given below.

	Steel	Aluminium
resistivity/Ω m	12×10^{-8}	3×10^{-8}
Young modulus/Pa	22×10^{10}	7×10^{10}
breaking stress/Pa	10×10^8	1×10^8

    (i) Show that, to a reasonable approximation, the electrical behaviour of the steel strands may be ignored. Hence, show that the resistance of 1 km of power line is $0.16\,\Omega$.

    (ii) Explain why the power line is operated at high voltage.

    (iii) Determine the percentage of the input power lost as heat per kilometre of the power line.

    (iv) Discuss the effect of the core of steel strands on the tensile properties of the line.

    (b) On the national grid operated at 132 kV r.m.s., power is usually transmitted from a three-phase generator, which generates three e.m.fs of equal amplitude separated in phase by 120°. The distribution of energy through the grid is made by four wires, one for each of the three phases (the phase wires) and one for the common return.

Using phasor diagrams, or otherwise, calculate

    (i) the difference in r.m.s. voltage between any two of the phase wires,

    (ii) the common return current if the loads on each phase are equal.

E10 Electrical transmission systems are designed so that the power lost in heating the cables is as low as possible. A projected system has cables of total resistance R and is supplied with an input power P.

(a) Find an expression for the power P_L delivered to a load if the input voltage is V.

(b) A certain power station provides an input power of 600 MW at an input voltage of 330 kV to a system of total cable resistance 0.90 Ω. If the efficiency η of the system is defined as P_L/P, what is η under these conditions?

(c) For a fixed input power, the efficiency can be increased by adjusting either the cable resistance or the input voltage. Discuss the practical and economic factors that should be considered in attempting to improve the efficiency in these ways.

E11 Define the 'farad' and show that the product of capacitance and resistance has the dimensions of time.

The potential difference V across a capacitor, which had previously been charged, was measured every 10 s. The results are tabulated below. At time $t = 15.0$ s, a resistor of 1.30×10^6 Ω was permanently connected across the capacitor.

t/s	0	10	20	30	40	50	60
V/V	10.0	10.0	8.87	6.98	5.49	4.32	3.40

(a) Explain the inherent difficulty in measuring this potential difference V. What kind of instrument would you use?

(b) Find the capacitance of the capacitor.

E12 (a) In Fig. E12.1, v_i^* represents the input voltage and v_c represents the output voltage across the capacitor.

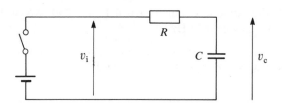

Fig. E12.1

Show that

$$RC(dv_c/dt) = v_i - v_c.$$

Hence show that, if v_i is held constant, the variation of v_c with time t is given by

$$v_c = v_i + A \exp(-t/RC),$$

where A is a constant that depends on the value of v_c at $t = 0$.

Hence show that, if the switch is closed at $t = 0$ with the capacitor uncharged,

$$v_c = v_i[1 - \exp(-t/RC)].$$

(b) The battery and switch in Fig. E12.1 are replaced by an oscillator, so that v_i has the form of a square wave of amplitude V_0 and period T, as shown in Fig. E12.2.

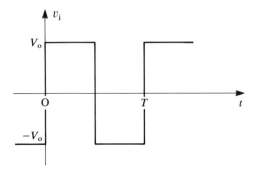

Fig. E12.2

Sketch and explain the time variation of v_c, drawing separate sketches for each of the three cases when $T \gg RC$, $T = RC$ and $T \ll RC$ respectively.

Show that v_c oscillates between values of $+V$ and $-V$, where

$$(V/V_0) = [1 - \exp(-T/RC)]/[1 + \exp(-T/RC)].$$

Calculate the minimum value of RC if V is not to exceed $0.01\ V_0$ for frequencies down to $1\ \text{kHz}$.

*Although this is not the normal symbol for potential difference, it has been used here to help distinguish the two parts of the question.)

E13 Show that, when an initially uncharged capacitor and a resistor are connected in series across a source of e.m.f., the charge on the capacitor at a given time later is a fixed fraction of the final charge on the capacitor irrespective of the applied voltage.

A capacitor C is charged to a potential V_0 and is then connected across two resistors R_A and R_B in series. R_B is shunted by a diode that limits the p.d. across itself to $V_0/5$ and conducts no current if the p.d. across it is less than $V_0/5$. What relationship between R_A and R_B must be satisfied if the diode is to conduct at all?

If $R_A = 2R_B$, calculate the time for which the diode conducts.

Draw graphs showing the variation with time of the currents through R_A, R_B and the diode.

E14 A square wave pulse of peak value 5 V and duration 0.02 s (see Fig. E14.1) is applied across a series combination of a 2 kΩ resistor and a 5 μF capacitor.

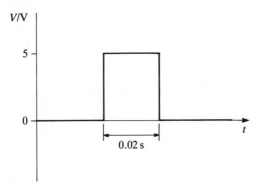

Fig. E14.1

Sketch as accurately as you can (taking into account the time constant of the combination but without performing other detailed calculations) the output voltage pulses across the resistor and capacitor respectively.

Show that, at any time, V_R and V_C are related by

$$V_R = RC\,dV_C/dt.$$

Fig. E14.2 shows a capacitor of capacitance C and a resistor of resistance R connected in series. An (inverting) operational amplifier is connected across the resistor. The input voltage V_{in} varies with time.

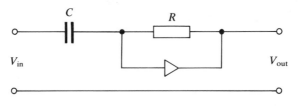

Fig. E14.2

Show that the output voltage is proportional to the rate of change of the input voltage. (This circuit is called a differentiating circuit.)

The resistor and capacitor are then interchanged as shown in Fig. E14.3. Find a relation between V_{out} and V_{in} and explain in words the function of the circuit.

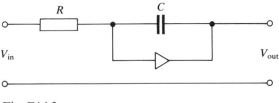

Fig. E14.3

Suggest an application for these types of circuit.

E15 A capacitor C and resistor R are connected in series. Explain what is meant by, and find an expression for, the *time constant* of this combination.

An alternating e.m.f. is applied to the combination. Find expressions for (a) the phase angle between the potential difference across the capacitor and the current flowing in it, (b) the power factor of this circuit.

A coil of N turns each of area A is rotating at a uniform angular velocity ω about an axis perpendicular to a uniform magnetic field of flux density B and connected via slip rings to a capacitor C and resistor R in series. Derive an expression for the instantaneous current when the coil is at an angle θ to the field and show that the average rate of working is

$$\frac{\omega^2 N^2 A^2 B^2 R}{2(R^2 + 1/\omega^2 C^2)}.$$

[Neglect the resistance and inductance of the rotating coil.]

E16* Figure E16.1 shows a simple relaxation oscillator, as used in a portable flashing hazard light.

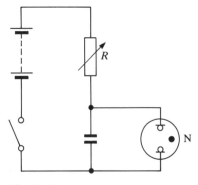

Fig. E16.1

A simplified explanation of the operation of the circuit is as follows: N is a neon lamp, which is non-conducting until the potential difference across it rises to 45 V. A discharge then takes place in the gas, reducing the resistance of the lamp effectively to zero, so that the capacitor discharges. The lamp then becomes non-conducting again, and the cycle repeats.

In a particular circuit, the e.m.f. of the battery is 90 V and the capacitance of the capacitor is 0.20 µF. What value of the resistor R would be required to obtain a flashing frequency of 2.0 Hz? Under these conditions, what is the mean power drawn from the battery?

E17* The current I in a glowing neon tube may be represented by

$$I/A = 1.31 \times 10^{-4}(V/V - 147)$$

for potentials above 157 V, below which there is no discharge. The neon tube is connected across a 50 µF capacitor, which has been charged to a potential of 220 V, a p.d. more than sufficient to initiate the discharge. For how long will the neon tube glow?

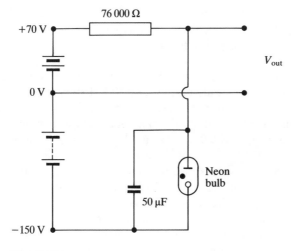

Fig. E17.1

A circuit is arranged as shown in Fig. E17.1. Given that the neon tube strikes when the potential across it reaches 210 V and that the batteries have low internal resistance, draw a sketch graph to show the approximate variation with time of V_{out}. Indicate the limits of the voltage variations and the order of magnitude of the time intervals involved.

E18 (a) Starting from Ohm's law, derive an expression for the electrical conductivity of a material in terms of the applied electric field and the resultant current density.

(b) In the classical theory of electrical conduction, the free electrons in a metal are supposed to behave like the molecules of an ideal gas. Each electron may be supposed to be accelerated by the applied electric field until it collides with a lattice ion, when the electron velocity is reduced to zero. The process of acceleration and collision is then repeated.

The conductivity of copper at room temperature is $5.6 \times 10^7 \, \Omega^{-1} \, m^{-1}$ and the number of free electrons per unit volume is $8.3 \times 10^{28} \, m^{-3}$. By writing down two expressions for the drift velocity, or otherwise, deduce the mean time between the collisions of the electrons with the copper ions.

(c) Besides moving with the drift velocity, the free electrons also experience random thermal motion. Estimate the average thermal speed of free electrons in copper at room temperature, assuming them to behave like the atoms of an ideal gas. Hence deduce the average distance λ travelled by the electrons between collisions with copper ions.

Comment on your value for λ and indicate how this model explains the experimental fact that the thermal conductivity of copper decreases with increasing temperature.

E19 (a) A copper wire of length 0.50 m and area of cross-section $2.0 \, mm^2$ is used to carry a steady current of 0.10 A. Estimate the time taken for a free electron to move from one end of the wire to the other.

[Assume that each atom of copper provides one free electron. The density of copper is $9.0 \times 10^3 \, kg \, m^{-3}$ and its relative atomic mass is 64.]

(b) If the same wire is used to carry an *alternating* current of peak value 0.10 A and frequency 50 Hz, estimate the amplitude of oscillation of free electrons in the wire.

(c)* An electrical signal, e.g. a pulse of charge, is suddenly applied at one end of the wire. Estimate how long it will be before the signal appears at the other end. Explain your answer and any connection it may have with the other estimates you have made.

Section EM

Electromagnetism

EM1 Two long thin parallel wires in a vacuum are separated by 0.20 m. They carry equal alternating currents of 3.0 A r.m.s. at 50 Hz. The currents are in phase. Sketch a graph to show how F, the force per unit length between the wires, varies with time t. Label the axes with appropriate numerical values.

EM2 A rectangular loop of wire of dimensions 10 cm by 20 cm and a long straight wire are in the same horizontal plane. The rectangular loop is positioned with its long sides parallel to the straight wire and with its nearer side 5 cm from it. The straight wire carries a current of 1.0 A. If there is a steady current of 0.15 A in the loop, so that the current in the side nearer the straight wire flows in the same direction as the current in the straight wire, discuss quantitatively the forces acting on the loop and indicate the way in which the loop will tend to move.

The current in the straight wire is reduced steadily to zero in 0.01 s. Calculate the magnitude of the e.m.f. induced in the loop and indicate its direction.

EM3* Two long straight parallel metal rods are supported with their axes a distance D apart; the radius r of each rod is very much less than D. The rods carry equal currents I in opposite directions, as shown in Fig. EM3.1. P is a point on the line RS in the plane of the rods, a distance y from one of them.

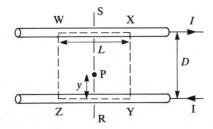

Fig. EM3.1

(a) Find the magnetic flux density B at the point P due to the currents in the rods. Hence find the total magnetic flux in the area WXYZ in Fig. EM3.1, where $WX = L$ and $XY = D$. (Assume that there is no flux in the rods themselves.)

(b) Hence find the self-inductance per unit length of the rods.

EM4* State how the magnetic flux density varies with distance from a long straight wire carrying current. Deduce how the magnetic flux density varies both inside and outside a thick wire carrying current uniformly distributed over the cross-section of the wire.

At very high frequencies, an alternating current carried by a wire flows in a very thin layer at the surface. Sketch a graph showing how the magnetic flux density both inside and outside the wire varies with the distance from the axis of the wire.

Assuming that the radius of the wire is a and that the current density is uniform over a distance x from the surface of the wire and zero elsewhere, find the ratio of the power dissipated in this high-frequency condition to that which would be dissipated if the same total current were uniformly distributed across the wire.

EM5* Find the magnetic flux density at the centre of a gramophone record of radius 0.15 m rotating at 33.3 revolutions per minute when a charge of 1.0 μC is distributed uniformly over its surface. What is the direction of the associated magnetic field?

Would your value be changed if the record were made of a non-magnetic but good conducting material such as copper?

EM6 A wire of fixed length l carries a constant current I. The wire is formed into a square coil and placed in a magnetic field of uniform flux density B. Show that the torque developed is a maximum when the coil has one turn only and find the value of this maximum torque.

EM7 A square coil of side a, consisting of N turns, rotates at angular frequency ω about an axis parallel to one of its sides in a uniform magnetic flux density B perpendicular to the axis of rotation. Show that an alternating voltage of amplitude $\omega a^2 N B$ is produced.

A rotating coil is to be used to measure a low magnetic flux density. The volume of wire used for the turns of the coil must not exceed V. The resistivity of the wire is ρ. The coil is connected to an ammeter of resistance R_m, which is able to measure currents down to a minimum value of I_{min}. Show that the minimum measurable magnetic flux density is given by

$$B_{\min} = I_{\min}(R_{\mathrm{m}}/N + 16\omega a^2 N/V)/a^2\rho.$$

Draw a sketch graph to show how $B_{\min}$ varies with N. What value of N should be used to give the highest sensitivity?

EM8 Explain the following.

(a) A resistor that is wound inductively passes less alternating current at a fixed potential difference than a resistor of the same resistance that is wound non-inductively.

(b) The current passed by the inductive resistor falls if the frequency is increased.

*A certain meter for measuring radio frequency alternating voltages depends for its action on the heating effect of the small alternating current passing through it. The meter is calibrated at 1 MHz. If the meter is equivalent to a resistor of resistance $10\,\mathrm{k}\Omega$ and an inductor of inductance 1 mH in series, over what range of frequencies will the calibration remain good to 5%?

EM9 A straight metal rod 50 cm long can slide with negligible friction on parallel conducting rails. It moves at right angles to a magnetic field of flux density 0.72 T. The rails are joined to a battery of e.m.f. 3.0 V and a fixed series resistor of value $1.6\,\Omega$; other resistances can be neglected. Find (a) the force required to hold the rod at rest, (b) the maximum speed the rod attains when released.

EM10 A cylindrical magnet with its axis vertical provides a radial magnetic field. A thin circular aluminium ring that is coaxial with the magnet falls through the magnetic field as shown in elevation in Fig. EM10.1.

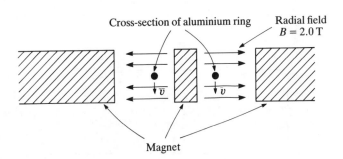

Fig. EM10.1

By first finding an expression for the current in the ring when it is falling at speed v, deduce the final constant velocity of the ring, if the magnetic flux density at the circumference of the ring is 2.0 T.

[For aluminium, resistivity $= 3.1 \times 10^{-8} \,\Omega\,\text{m}$, and density $= 2.7 \times 10^3 \,\text{kg}\,\text{m}^{-3}$.]

EM11 A locomotive travels due magnetic west at $120 \,\text{km}\,\text{h}^{-1}$. Explain why the potential difference between the centre and the rim of the wheels, as would be measured by a stationary observer, varies round the rim. If the diameter of a wheel is 1.6 m and the horizontal component of the Earth's magnetic flux density is $1.76 \times 10^{-5} \,\text{T}$, calculate the maximum potential difference and say where this will occur.

EM12 Discuss briefly the application of the laws of electromagnetic induction to a circular coil of wire that is being unwound while its axis is along the Earth's magnetic meridian.

A long solenoid of radius r is wound with N turns per unit length. Near its centre is mounted a copper disc of radius a ($a < r$) so that the axes of the disc and solenoid coincide. A spring penetrates through a small hole in the solenoid and makes good electrical contact with the circumference of the disc. An oscilloscope, suitably arranged to indicate voltage, is connected between the spring and a brush resting on the conducting axle of the disc beyond the end of the solenoid.

An alternating current $I = I_0 \sin \omega t$ passes through the solenoid. Discuss what will be the voltage indicated (a) when the disc rotates at n revolutions per second, (b) when the disc is stationary.

EM13 Starting from the definitions of capacitance and inductance, derive an expression for the natural frequency of oscillation of a capacitor and inductor in parallel.

In the circuit shown in Fig. EM13.1, S_1 and S_2 are electronic switches, which may be opened rapidly. Initially, the switches are open, capacitor C_1 is uncharged and capacitor C_2 is charged to 100 V. Describe in detail, and explain, the sequence of operations required to charge capacitor C_1 to 200 V.

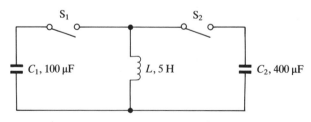

Fig. EM13.1

EM14 A particular metal can be made to have zero resistance (i.e. it becomes superconducting) if it is taken below a certain very low temperature. At higher temperatures, the metal behaves normally.

A superconducting solenoid of inductance 60 mH is connected in series with a 12 V d.c. supply of negligible internal resistance. At a time 0.5 s after the connection of this supply, the solenoid suddenly loses its superconducting property and reverts to its normal state with resistance 20 Ω.

(a) Determine how the current I in the superconducting solenoid varies with time t.

(b) Display your results on a sketch graph, showing appropriate values of current and time. Indicate on your graph how the current changes with time when the solenoid has reverted to its normal state.

EM15 A long solenoid of length l and radius r has n turns per unit length. A uniform magnetic field of flux density B exists within the solenoid when there is a current I in its coils.

(a) Write down the relation between B and I and hence find an expression for the self-inductance L of the solenoid in terms of l, n, r and μ_0, the permeability of a vacuum.

(b) The energy U stored in the field of an inductor carrying a current I is given by $U = LI^2/2$. Use the dimensions or base units of the quantities involved to show that this equation is dimensionally consistent.

(c) The wire of the solenoid is of resistivity ρ and cross-sectional area A. If the ends of the solenoid are suddenly short-circuited, find an expression for the time taken for the flux density within the solenoid to fall to B/e. (e is the base of natural logarithms.)

EM16* A piece of wire 8.0 cm long, of resistance 0.020 Ω and mass 22 mg, is bent to form a closed square ABCD. It is mounted so as to turn without friction about a horizontal axis through AB; a uniform horizontal magnetic field of flux density 0.50 T is applied at right angles to the axis. The side CD is raised until the plane of the square is horizontal and then released. Calculate approximately the time taken for the plane of the square to become vertical. You can assume that, during the falling, the couple due to gravity is equal and opposite to that due to electromagnetic forces.

EM17 A copper disc of radius a is placed inside a large solenoid so that the axes of disc and solenoid coincide. The solenoid has n turns per unit length and a total resistance R, and is orientated along the Earth's magnetic field, which has a flux density B_0. One end of the solenoid is connected to the rim of the disc and the other end to the centre of the disc via a suitable ammeter. The disc is rotated with gradually increasing speed up to a speed short of that which would cause breaking. This is done first in one direction and then in the other. Continuous observations are made of the current in the circuit. Discuss and explain these observations and derive an expression for any speed that is of special interest.

EM18* Fig. EM18.1 shows a simple spring made of wire of negligible mass and containing only two turns, each of radius 12 mm. It is fixed at its upper end. When no load is attached to the lower end, the separation of the coils is d.

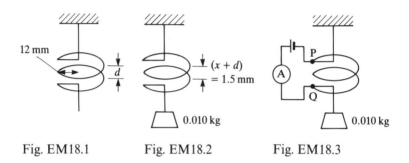

Fig. EM18.1 Fig. EM18.2 Fig. EM18.3

When a load of mass 0.010 kg is fixed to the lower end, as in Fig. EM18.2, the spring extends so that the distance $(d + x)$ between the turns is then 1.5 mm.

A battery is then connected between the points P and Q, as shown in Fig. EM18.3. The current in the coils is 6.2 A. A very small change Δx in the distance between the coils is noted. Find the fractional change $\Delta x/x$.

[Assume that the electrical connections to the spring cause no additional load, and that the spring obeys Hooke's law.]

EM19 The magnetic flux density in a long solenoid of length l and total turns N when a current I is flowing is

$$B = \mu_0 N I / l.$$

The cross-sectional area of the solenoid is A.

(a) By first finding the flux linking the circuit, obtain the e.m.f. induced in the solenoid when the current changes at the rate of dI/dt.

(b) Hence find the self-inductance of the solenoid.

*A vertical helical spring, of negligible mass and of radius 1.0 cm, has 1000 turns per metre and carries a current I. If the coil is stretched so that its length increases by a small amount δl, find expressions for

(c) the change in magnetic energy of the coil,

(d) the work done on the battery.

Hence find the value of I required to restore the coil to its original length when a mass of 2.0 g is hung on the end.

EM20 An alternating current is represented by the equation

$$I = I_0 \sin \omega t.$$

Write down (a) the r.m.s. (root-mean-square) value of the current, (b) the frequency of the current. Deduce the maximum value of the rate of change of the current.

A long solenoid wound with 10^3 turns per metre carries an alternating current of frequency 50 Hz and of r.m.s. value 1.0 A. In the centre of the solenoid is mounted coaxially a five-turn coil of diameter 1.0 cm. Calculate the r.m.s. voltage induced in this coil.

If the inner coil is surrounded by a copper tube, the voltage induced in it decreases. Explain this result.

EM21 A moving-coil loudspeaker has a cylindrical coil of diameter 2.0 cm with 40 turns, mounted in a radial magnetic field of flux density 1.2 T. If the effective mass of the moving system is 4.0 g, what is the amplitude of movement when a sinusoidal current of root-mean-square value 0.10 A at 1000 Hz flows through the coil? Neglect elastic forces due to the suspension.

EM22 A designer builds a transformer to operate an X-ray unit at 80 kV peak and 250 mA r.m.s. (root-mean-square) from the normal 240 V r.m.s. supply. He makes no allowance for the possibility of lead resistance between the mains and the unit. If there were a mains cable resistance of 0.5 Ω after installation, what supply voltage would be required instead of 240 V to maintain the same operating conditions?

EM23 Show that, for a loss-free transformer with a resistive load, (a) the ratio of the primary p.d. to the secondary p.d. is equal to the ratio of the number of turns of the primary to that of the secondary (i.e. the turns ratio), (b) the ratio of the current in the primary to the secondary current is approximately equal to the reciprocal of the turns ratio.

Derive a formula for the turns ratio required to match a generator, having an internal resistance of R_p, to a load of R_s so that maximum power is transferred to the load.

Explain why transformers for radio frequencies have air or dust–iron cores.

EM24 In a cathode-ray tube with magnetic deflection, a deflecting field of 1.0×10^{-3} T is applied uniformly over a cylindrical volume of radius 50 mm in a direction parallel to the axis of the cylinder: elsewhere, the field is zero. The electron beam enters the field along a radius of the cylinder.

Describe, with the aid of a diagram, the subsequent path of the electrons. Calculate the speed if the beam undergoes a total deflection of $20°$.

EM25 Cathode rays are accelerated in a cathode-ray tube by a potential difference V applied between the cathode and final anode. The tube in placed inside a long solenoid so that the cathode rays emitted are parallel to the magnetic field. An electrostatic field is now applied by small Y-plates, giving the rays a component of velocity at right angles to the magnetic field. The magnetic field intensity H is now adjusted so that the electrons follow a helical path and make one complete revolution in the distance d between the Y-plates and the screen.

Show that the ratio of charge e to mass m_e for the electron is

$$\frac{e}{m_e} = \frac{KV}{H^2 d^2},$$

where K is a constant.

EM26 A cathode-ray tube has deflector plates of length x (measured parallel to the axis of the tube). The potential difference across the electron gun is V. A sinusoidal potential difference of constant amplitude but variable frequency is applied across the deflector plates. As the frequency is increased, the length of the line on the tube face decreases, first becoming zero at frequency f. By considering the time spent by an electron between the deflector plates, derive an expression for the ratio of charge e to mass m_e for the electron in terms of x, V and f.

What happens if the frequency is increased further?

EM27* Two large metal plates are held vertical and parallel to each other with a horizontal separation of 2 m. The potential difference between the plates is 200 V and there is a vertical magnetic flux density of 1×10^{-5} T.

Given that a proton leaves the centre of the positive plates with zero velocity at time $t = 0$, calculate (a) when, (b) where, it will strike the other plate. You may assume that the deflection of the proton in this weak magnetic field will be small.

Explain, without calculation, how the motion would be affected by a stronger magnetic field.

EM28 A narrow beam of positive ions passes through a region of length L, where it is acted on by an electric field of intensity E and a magnetic field of flux density B. The two fields are parallel to each other but perpendicular to the path of the ions. After passing through a further distance D ($\gg L$) of field-free space, the ions strike a fluorescent screen. Show that, for small deflections, ions that are identical in mass m and in charge q but differ in their speeds, generate a parabolic trace on the screen.

Deduce order-of-magnitude estimates of the field intensities required for such an experiment.

EM29 Radio emission from the Milky Way may be due to the acceleration of high-energy electrons as they move in spiral paths in the interstellar magnetic field. Here you will work through a simplified model of this process.

An electron enters a region of uniform magnetic field of flux density B of 1.2×10^{-3} T with an initial velocity v of 3.0×10^7 m s^{-1} at an angle of $30°$ to the magnetic field. Thereafter, it moves in a helix of radius r and pitch p, the axis of the helix being parallel to the directions of the field, as shown in Fig. EM29.1.

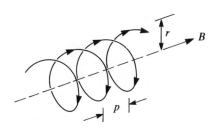

Fig. EM29.1

(a) Explain why the electron moves in a helix.

(b) Calculate r. Find also the time for the electron to travel along one complete turn of the helix. Hence find p.

(c) Find the wavelength of the radio emission associated with this electron motion.

M30 (a) A Hall-effect probe is made from a rectangular strip of a semiconducting material 0.120 mm thick. The probe is placed in a uniform magnetic field of flux density 1.10×10^{-2} T, and a current of 80 mA is passed through it, as shown in Fig. EM30.1. The potential of the point Z relative to that of Y is found to be $+114\,\text{mV}$.

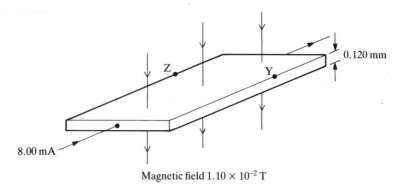

Fig. EM30.1

Deduce the sign of the charge on the charge carriers in the semiconductor, and calculate the number density of the charge carriers. Assume that the magnitude of the charge on each carrier is $1.6 \times 10^{-19}\,\text{C}$.

(b) Hall-effect probes may be used to measure magnetic flux density. Explain why semiconductors are used in such probes in preference to metals.

Section A

Atomic and nuclear physics

A1 How may (i) the intensity, (ii) the penetrating power, of the X-rays emitted by a modern X-ray tube be controlled?

Such a tube is operating with an anode potential of 10 kV and an anode current of 15.0 mA.

(a) Estimate the number of electrons hitting the anode per second.

(b) Calculate the rate of production of heat at the anode, stating any assumptions made.

(c) Describe the characteristics of the emitted X-ray spectrum and account for any special features.

A2 Fig. A2.1, which is not to scale, shows a simplified picture of the electron energy levels in a certain atom. The zero of energy represents the energy of an electron at rest at an infinite distance from the nucleus.

The atom is bombarded with high-energy electrons. In Fig. A2.2,

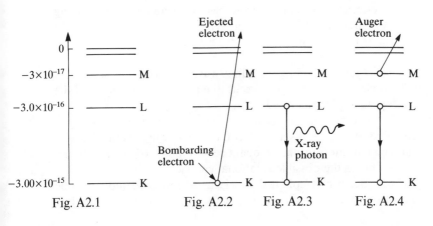

Fig. A2.1   Fig. A2.2   Fig. A2.3   Fig. A2.4

the impact of one of these electrons has caused the ejection of an electron from the level labelled K and its complete removal from the atom. The vacant place in the K-level is then filled by an electron from the L-level, with a certain amount of energy being released in this transition. The energy may appear either as a photon of electromagnetic radiation in the X-ray region of the spectrum (Fig. A2.3), or it may all be used to eject an M-level electron from the atom, as shown in Fig. A2.4. (This latter process is called Auger electron emission.)

(a) Through what minimum potential difference must a bombarding electron be accelerated from rest to cause the ejection of a K-electron from the atom?

(b) How much energy is released when the L-electron moves to fill the vacancy in the K-level?

(c) Calculate the wavelength of X-rays as emitted in Fig. A2.3.

(d) Calculate the kinetic energy of an Auger electron emitted from the M-level, as in Fig. A2.4.

A3 A small mass m, having a charge of e, moves in a circular orbit around a larger stationary mass of charge $-e$. If the angular momentum of the small mass is $h/2\pi$, derive an expression for the total energy in terms of m, e and h, and hence find the energy change that occurs if the angular momentum changes abruptly to h/π (gravitational effects may be ignored).

A4 What does it mean to say that a certain physical quantity is quantised? A particle of mass m with wave-like properties is confined to move on a line between two points distance L apart. Only modes of motion that produce a standing wave pattern between the points are allowed. Show that the momentum of the particle can only take values $nh/2L$, where n is an integer. Hence find the possible values of the kinetic energy.

In a certain fluorescent molecule, electrons can move freely along a carbon chain 1.1×10^{-9} m long. What colour light is emitted in transitions between the fourth and third energy levels?

A5 (a) Show that, if a simple standing wave pattern were associated with an electron orbiting a nucleus, the angular momentum of the electron would be quantised in units of $h/2\pi$.

(b) A diatomic gas molecule consists of two atoms of mass m separated by a fixed distance d. If the atoms rotate as in Fig. A5.1 and angular momentum is quantised in units of $h/2\pi$, find an expression for the possible rotational energies.

(c) An electron is confined by electrical forces to move in one dimension between two barriers 1×10^{-9} m apart. If only standing

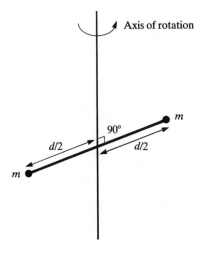

Fig. A5.1

waves are allowed, find the kinetic energy of the three lowest electron energy levels.

Explain, with an appropriate calculation, why energy quantisation is unimportant for a $10\,\mu g$ speck of dust bouncing between two walls $0.1\,mm$ apart at a speed of $1 \times 10^{-6}\,m\,s^{-1}$.

A6* The density of liquid hydrogen is $90\,kg\,m^{-3}$.

(a) Estimate the radius of the hydrogen atom.

(b) Assuming that the electron in a hydrogen atom moves in a circular orbit of this radius, calculate (i) its angular velocity, (ii) its total energy.

(c) According to classical electromagnetic theory, a charge e travelling in a circular orbit of radius a with angular velocity ω should radiate energy at a rate of $e^2a^2\omega^4/3\pi\varepsilon_0 c$. Estimate the classical lifetime of the hydrogen atom, i.e. the time it should take for an electron to spiral in and hit the proton.

A7 A nucleus of nucleon (mass) number 20 is travelling at $3 \times 10^5\,m\,s^{-1}$ when it disintegrates spontaneously into two particles, each of nucleon number 10, which fly apart at right angles to each other. Find the increase in kinetic energy.

Where does this energy come from?

A8* An α-particle travelling at $5.0 \times 10^5\,m\,s^{-1}$ makes a head-on collision with another α-particle that is initially stationary but free to move. What is the theoretical closest distance of approach of the two particles?

A9 Uncharged monoenergetic particles make head-on elastic collisions with stationary protons or α-particles. Calculate the ratio

$$\frac{\text{kinetic energy of protons}}{\text{kinetic energy of }\alpha\text{-particles}}$$

after collisions if the incident particles are
  (a) heavy particles of mass equal to that of a proton,
  (b) quanta of electromagnetic radiation.
[Assume that the speeds of all particles other than quanta of electromagnetic radiation are very much less than the speed of electromagnetic waves.]

A10 The line of flight of a certain α-particle incident on a thin gold foil passes a distance p from a certain gold nucleus.
  (a) Use the law of conservation of angular momentum to relate d, the closest distance of approach of the α-particle to the nucleus, to u_0, its initial velocity, u_m, its minimum velocity, and p.
  (b) By also using the law of conservation of energy, show that an α-particle with initial energy E will pass within a distance d of a gold nucleus only if its initial line of flight passes within a distance $d\,[(E-V)/E]^{1/2}$ of that nucleus, where V is the potential energy of the α-particle when it is a distance d from a gold nucleus.
  (c) Hence find the fraction of incident monoenergetic α-particles passing within a distance d of a gold nucleus in terms of d, E, V, x and N, where x is the foil thickness and N the number of gold nuclei per unit volume.
[Assume $d \ll$ interatomic spacing and that the gold nuclei remain stationary.]

A11 A copper sphere, suspended by an insulating thread in a vacuum, is illuminated by monochromatic radiation of wavelength 150 nm. What is the maximum potential the sphere could reach by losing photoelectrons? Explain your reasoning carefully.
  In practice, when a metal is illuminated by monochromatic radiation, it is found that electrons are emitted with a range of energies. Suggest reasons for this.
[Work function of copper, $\phi = 4.5$ V.]

A12 Fig. A12.1 shows a metal plate M of work function ϕ. A luminescent screen S (similar to the screen in a cathode-ray tube) is mounted parallel to M and a distance y from it. The arrangement is contained in an evacuated tube.
  A very small area P of the metal plate is illuminated with monochromatic light of wavelength λ, such that photoelectrons are emitted from the plate. The screen is at a positive potential V with

respect to M, so that the photoelectrons are accelerated towards the screen. When the electrons strike the screen, their kinetic energy is converted to light energy. It is found that the electrons emitted from the area P produce a bright disc D of radius r on the luminescent screen.

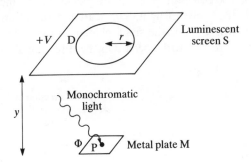

Fig. A12.1

(a) Find an expression for the maximum speed v_m with which a photoelectron can leave the surface.

(b) A certain electron E leaves P with velocity v_m in a direction that grazes the metal surface, as shown in Fig. A12.2. How long does it take this electron to reach the screen? Give your answer in terms of y, V, the electron mass m_e and the elementary charge e.

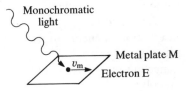

Fig. A12.2

(c) Hence find the radius r of the bright disc on the screen. Explain your reasoning.

(d) In an experiment with an accelerating potential difference of 100 V, the radius of the bright disc is found to be 20 mm. What would be the radius if the accelerating potential were increased to 400 V?

A13 When X-ray photons are incident on a graphite target, it is observed that some of the scattered radiation is of longer wavelength (lower frequency) than the incident beam; the larger the angle through which the X-rays are scattered, the greater the change in wavelength. This phenomenon is called the *Compton effect*. In this question, you will work through a simplified derivation of the theory of the effect.

An incident X-ray photon is scattered by an electron, initially at rest (see Fig. A13.1). The momentum of the incident photon is hf/c, where h is the Planck constant, f is the frequency of the incident radiation and c is the speed of light. The scattered radiation is of frequency $f - \Delta f$, where Δf is the small change of frequency. The electron, of mass m_e, recoils with speed v in the direction shown.

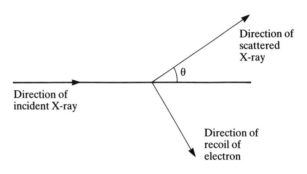

Fig. A13.1

(a) Use the principle of conservation of momentum to draw a labelled vector diagram relating the momentum before to the momentum after this interaction.

(b) Hence obtain an expression for the momentum $m_e v$ of the recoil electron in terms of h, f, Δf, c and θ.

(c) Use the principle of conservation of energy to write down an energy equation for this interaction.

(d) Hence show that the change in wavelength $\Delta \lambda$ of the scattered radiation is given approximately by

$$\Delta \lambda \approx h(1 - \cos \theta)/m_e c.$$

(e) Sketch a graph showing how $\Delta \lambda$ depends on θ, for values of θ between $0°$ and $180°$. For what value of θ is $\Delta \lambda$ a maximum? Give a physical explanation of why the maximum change of wavelength might be expected to occur at this angle.

A14   The positron is a fundamental particle with the same mass as that of the electron and with a charge equal to that of the electron but of opposite sign. When a positron and electron collide, they may annihilate each other. The energy corresponding to their mass appears in two photons of equal energy. Calculate the energy of one photon in electron-volts and the wavelength of the radiation.

A15 In the vicinity of a heavy atomic nucleus a γ-ray may be converted into an electron and a positron (β-particles of equal mass but opposite charge).

The frequency of such a γ-ray is 2.50×10^{20} Hz. Neglecting energy imparted to the nucleus and assuming that the speeds of the β-particles are equal, what is their speed?

What is the maximum total momentum the β-particles can have? Hence show that the presence of the nucleus is essential for momentum conservation.

A16 A stationary atom of uranium-238 disintegrates into thorium-234 with the emission of an α-particle. Give an equation to represent this reaction and use the data below to calculate the kinetic energy of the α-particle.

[Atomic mass of $^{238}\text{U} = 238.124\,92\,m_\text{u}$; atomic mass of $^{234}\text{Th} = 234.116\,50\,m_\text{u}$; atomic mass of $^{4}\text{He} = 4.003\,87\,m_\text{u}$.]

A17 Explain why the decay of radioactive material obeys an exponential law.

The age of a piece of wood is to be determined by measuring the radioactivity of the carbon-14 it contains. The proportion of carbon-14 atoms to natural carbon-12 atoms in living wood is about 1.25 to 10^{12}. When the wood dies, the carbon-14 decays with a half-life of 5600 years. If the number of disintegrations measured from 10.0 g of carbon prepared from a piece of wood is 48 per minute, estimate the age of the wood.

[1 year $= 3.16 \times 10^{7}$ s.]

A18 The uranium nuclide $^{238}_{92}\text{U}$ decays naturally by a series of stages to the lead nuclide $^{206}_{82}\text{Pb}$. Two schemes for the decay are suggested:

$$^{238}_{92}\text{U} \rightarrow {}^{206}_{82}\text{Pb} + 10\text{p} + 22\text{n};$$

$$^{238}_{92}\text{U} \rightarrow {}^{206}_{82}\text{Pb} + 8{}^{4}_{2}\text{He} + 6\text{e}^{-}.$$

The total binding energy of ^{238}U is 1801 MeV, that of ^{206}Pb is 1613 MeV and that of ^{4}He is 28.3 MeV. Discuss quantitatively the energy balance of the two schemes, and comment on their feasibilities.

The nuclide ^{235}U also decays naturally by a different scheme. The present-day abundances of ^{238}U and ^{235}U are in the ratio 137.8:1. Assuming that an equal amount of each isotope existed in the Earth's crust at the time of its formation, estimate the age of the Earth, given that the half-lives are as follows:

$$^{238}_{92}\text{U}, 4.5 \times 10^{9} \text{ years}; {}^{235}_{92}\text{U}, 7.13 \times 10^{8} \text{ years}.$$

A19 A sample of radioactive element decays into a stable nuclide with decay constant λ. Show that N_s, the number of stable atoms at time t, is related to N_t, the number of radioactive atoms remaining at time t, by the equation

$$N_s = N_t(e^{\lambda t} - 1).$$

(Sketch on the same graph the time variations of N_s and N_t.)

In one of the decay chains that occurs in nature, ^{238}U (which has a half-life of 4.5×10^9 years) decays eventually to stable ^{206}Pb, while in another ^{235}U (which has a half-life of 0.7×10^9 years) decays to ^{207}Pb.

Determine the numbers of alpha and negative beta particles emitted when one nucleus of ^{238}U decays to ^{206}Pb and when one nucleus of ^{235}U decays to ^{207}Pb.

To estimate the age of a certain rock sample, its present-day composition is measured. $N_{206}/N_{207} = 14$, where N_{206} and N_{207} are the numbers of (stable) atoms of ^{206}Pb and ^{207}Pb. $N_{238}/N_{235} = 138$, where N_{238} and N_{235} are the numbers of atoms of ^{238}U and ^{235}U. If all other radionuclides in the decay chains have much shorter half-lives than ^{238}U and ^{235}U and may thus be neglected, obtain an equation for t, the age of the sample.

Show, by substitution, that the equations are consistent with $t \approx 1 \times 10^9$ years.

What assumptions are made in this method for determining the age of the rock?

A20* When ^{61}Ni nuclei are bombarded with deuterons in a cyclotron, the positron emitter ^{61}Cu (which has a half-life of 3.3 h) is produced. If copper atoms are made at a rate of $5.0 \times 10^8 \, \mathrm{s}^{-1}$ while the cyclotron is running, what is the maximum mass of ^{61}Cu that can be produced?

If a fresh sample of ^{61}Ni is placed in the beam, when will the activity due to ^{61}Cu in the target reach 99% of its maximum value?

[The substitutions $y = a - bx$, $\mathrm{d}y/\mathrm{d}t = -b\,\mathrm{d}x/\mathrm{d}t$, where a and b are constants, may be useful. In $100 = 4.6$.]

A21 The steel compression ring for the piston of a car engine has a mass of 25 g. The ring is irradiated with neutrons until it has a uniformly distributed activity of 4×10^5 Bq due to the formation of ^{59}Fe. The ring is immediately installed in an engine. After the engine has been running for 30 days, a 100 cm^3 sample of the engine oil is taken out and 126 disintegrations are recorded from it during a 10 min counting period. If the total volume of oil is $5 \times 10^{-3} \, \mathrm{m}^3$, what fraction of the iron ring has worn away during this period? Assume that all metal worn away is in suspension in the oil.

[1 Bq = 1 disintegration per second; half-life of ^{59}Fe = 45 days.]

A22   In a slow reaction, heat is being evolved at a rate of about 10 mW in a liquid of mass 0.02 kg (specific heat capacity 4 kJ kg^{-1} K^{-1}). If a copper–constantan thermocouple with a thermoelectric power of 40 µV K^{-1} coupled to a galvanometer with a sensitivity of 1000 mm µA^{-1} and a resistance of 100 Ω are used to measure the rate of rise of temperature of the liquid, estimate the rate of movement of the galvanometer needle.

   If the heat were being generated by the decay of ^{32}P, a radioactive isotope of phosphorus that has a half-life of 14 days and emits only beta-particles with a mean energy of 700 keV, estimate the number of ^{32}P atoms in the liquid.

   [1 day = 8.6 × 10^4 s;   1 eV = 1.6 × 10^{-19} J.]

Answers

General physics, physical quantities and measurement techniques

G1 (c) and (d) are incorrect.

G2 (a) $R = (k\varepsilon_0 h^2)/(me^2)$, where k is a dimensionless constant; if $k = 1$,
$R = 1.7 \times 10^{-10}$ m;
(b) $(vR\eta)/\rho$; $F/(\rho v^2 R^2)$.

G3 $220 \,\text{V}\,\text{m}^{-1}$.

G4 $a = \text{L}\,\text{T}^{-2}$ or $\text{m}\,\text{s}^{-2}$; $b = \text{M}\,\text{T}^{-2}$ or $\text{kg}\,\text{s}^{-2}$; $\Delta b = -0.072 \,\text{kg}\,\text{s}^{-2}$.

G5 Exposure $= (0.0621 \pm 0.0007)\,\text{s}$ (nominally $0.0667\,\text{s}$).

G6 Magnitude of velocity $= (a^2\omega^2 + b^2)^{1/2}$;
magnitude of acceleration $= \omega^2 a$;
velocity and acceleration vectors are at right angles.

G7 $X_0 = (m_1 x_1 + m_2 x_2)/(m_1 + m_2)$; the force acts along the line $y = x$,
from the positive quadrant towards the origin.

G8 $T = 5\,\text{s} + \text{reaction time}$.

G9 (a) 1.32×10^4 m; (b) 12.8 m;
(c) 4.09×10^6 m; (d) 2.55 m.

G11 (a) 0; (b) -0.32%; (c) -0.32%.

G12 1.4×10^{-19} J.

G13 $n = 2$; $E_0 = 4.18\,\text{eV}$.

G14 $2.8\,\text{s}$; $49°$ to the tangent.

Mechanics and gravitation

M1 (a) $A = 0.19\,\text{kg}\,\text{m}^{-1}$; $B = 3.9\,\text{N}$;
(b) $5.8\,\text{m}\,\text{s}^{-1}$.

M2 (a) About $1 \times 10^4\,\text{N}$;
(b) about $1 \times 10^3\,\text{J}$;
(c) about $30\,\text{m}\,\text{s}^{-1}$.

M3 $0.68\,\text{m}$.

M4 $3.4 \times 10^5\,\text{km}$ from centre of Earth; $2.4\,\text{km}\,\text{s}^{-1}$.

M5 (a) $7.9 \times 10^3\,\text{m}\,\text{s}^{-1}$;
(d) $8.4 \times 10^6\,\text{m}$; $2.5 \times 10^3\,\text{m}\,\text{s}^{-1}$;
(e) $50\,\text{s}$ burn when at closest point.

M6 $1.1\,\text{s}$.

M7 M.

M8 $3Mg$.

M9 (b) (ii) 0.20;
(iii) fractional change in radius $= 1.3\%$.

M10 55 collisions; $1.4 \times 10^{-10}\,\text{m}$.

M11 The balance should be able to detect $0.06\,\text{N}$ in $10\,\text{N}$.

M12 $\omega = (2ag)^{1/2}$.

M13 $5.4\,\text{rad}\,\text{s}^{-1}$.

M14 $6.5\,\text{m}\,\text{s}^{-1}$.

M15   (a) $2\pi(d^3/3Gm)^{1/2}$;
      (c) the wavelength of the line will be 2.89 nm longer and, every 47
      days, it will split into two lines 0.11 nm apart.

M16   (a) (i) 18 kW; (ii) 144 kW;
      (b) about 1×10^9 W.

M18 $8000\,\text{m}\,\text{s}^{-1}$; about $2°3'\text{W}$ of N.

M19 $X = g/2\pi G\rho$.

M20 $g_{\text{lead}} = g + 4.7 \times 10^{-6}\,\text{m}\,\text{s}^{-2}$ (i.e. less than 0.5%).

M21 $M/2A\rho V$.

M22 $16\pi^2\rho^2 Gr^4\delta r/3; 3GM^2/5R$.

M23   (a) $10\,\text{m}\,\text{s}^{-2}$;
      (b) $3.3 \times 10^{10}\,\text{J}$;
      (c) $2.5 \times 10^{-2}\,\text{m}\,\text{s}^{-2}$.

M24 $1.25 \times 10^3\,\text{m}\,\text{s}^{-1}; 50\,\text{m}\,\text{s}^{-2}$.

M25   (a) $F = (p_0 y A)/(y_0 + y)$;
      (b) work done by gas in expanding $= p_0 A y_0(2 - \ln 3)$;
      work done in stretching spring $= (2p_0^2 A^2)/9k$.

M26   (a) $\omega = \Omega\exp[-(k/I)t]$;
      (c) $(I \ln 2)/k$.

Oscillations and waves, particularly light and sound

W1 1.1×10^5 photons.

W2 (c) λ (electron) $= 1.2 \times 10^{-11}$ m;
(d) light intensity fluctuates at a frequency $4f$.

W3 $2\pi\left(\dfrac{l}{g-a}\right)^{1/2}$; $2\pi\left(\dfrac{l}{(g^2+v^4/r^2)^{1/2}}\right)^{1/2}$; 1.992 N; 2.016 N.

W4 $a/3$.

W5 27.5 Hz; 1.2×10^{-19} J; 1.1×10^{-11} m.

W6 (a) Maximum reading $= 2M$ at $t = \pi(\alpha M/g)^{1/2}$;
(b) $\tau = \pi(M_0/g)^{1/2}(\alpha_1^{1/2} + \alpha_2^{1/2})$.

W7 $\dfrac{mg\sin\alpha}{k}$ below O.

W8 They are almost equal.

W10 1.7 mm; $0.015°$.

W11 4.62×10^{-7} m; 5.45×10^{-7} m; 6.67×10^{-7} m.

W12 $I_{max}/I_{min} = 9$; fringe separation $= 0.24$ mm.

W13 (a) $d(\sin\alpha - \sin\beta) = m\lambda$, where $m = 0, \pm 1, \ldots$;
(b) at angles β to the normal of $56.4°$, $30.0°$ and $9.6°$.

W14   (a) Centre, $\pm 0.4\,\text{mm}$, $\pm 0.8\,\text{mm}$;
   (b) Centre, $\pm 0.65\,\text{mm}$, $\pm 1.3\,\text{mm}$;
   pattern lost for $\lambda = 400\,\text{nm}$ when $\delta = 6 \times 10^{-5}\,\text{m}$ and for
   $\lambda = 650\,\text{nm}$ when $\delta = 9.8 \times 10^{-5}\,\text{m}$.

W15 $0.3\,\text{mm}$.

W16   Second and third orders only.

W17 $17.7°$

W18   (a) Violet, $404.9\,\text{nm}$; blue, $435.7\,\text{nm}$; green, $546.0\,\text{nm}$; yellow, $576.4\,\text{nm}$
   and $579.3\,\text{nm}$. A violet line will be observed at an angle of $70.9°$.

W19 $340\,\text{m s}^{-1}$; $29\,\text{m s}^{-1}$.

W20 $8.37 \times 10^{3}\,\text{m}$; $2.5 \times 10^{-10}\,\text{s}$.

W21 $0.45\,\text{m}$; $5 \times 10^{-3}\,\text{m s}^{-1}$; $0.1\,\text{Hz}$.

W22   Aircraft speed $= 85\,\text{m s}^{-1}$;
   difference in angular speeds of engines $= 24\,\text{rad s}^{-1}$.

W23 $29\,\text{m s}^{-1}$.

W24   Speed of spacecraft $1.65\,\text{km s}^{-1}$; speed of tracking station $0.27\,\text{km s}^{-1}$;
   radius of Earth $6000\,\text{km}$.

W25 $4(l/g)^{1/2}$.

W26 $6.25 \times 10^{-3}\,\text{m}$; $31.5n\,\text{Hz}$, where n is an odd integer.

W27   The $220\,\text{Hz}$ string emits the following frequencies: $440\,\text{Hz}$, $880\,\text{Hz}$, ...

W28   (a) $500\,\text{Hz}$; $1/2$;
   (c) $m^2/4$;
   (d) $0.99\,\text{MHz}$ to $1.01\,\text{MHz}$; 50.

W29 $D = 2\pi^{2}f^{2}A^{2}\rho$; $2 \times 10^{-10}\,\text{m}$.

States of matter

SM1 $1.46 \times 10^{-2}\,\text{m}$.

SM2 $2.4 \times 10^{-5}\,\text{m}^2$.

SM3   Yes–just!

SM4   (a) $L = H - (2MgH/k)^{1/2}$;
(b) Fig. SM4.1 is the answer.

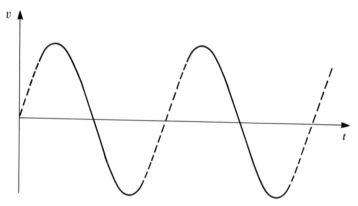

Fig. SM4.1

SM7   (a) Fig. SM7.1 is the answer.

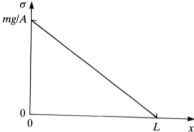

Fig. SM7.1

(b) Aluminium, copper, tungsten, tin, silver.

Answers

SM8 4.5×10^{-20} J.

SM9   (i) 1.2×10^{-10} m; (ii) 8×10^{-17} J; (iii) 1.1×10^{-14} Hz.

SM10   (a) $f_1 = (1/2\pi)(k/M)^{1/2}$;
       (c) $7.5\,\mu$m.

SM11   (e) $-4.7\,$aJ;
       (g) $0.4\,$aJ.

SM12 $6.01 \times 10^{23}\,$mol^{-1}.

SM13

	Number of ions	Distance from P
Na$^+$ ions like A	6	d
Cl$^-$ ions like B	12	$2^{1/2}d$
Na$^+$ ions like C	8	$3^{1/2}d$

$V_{es} = -2.1\,e^2/(4\pi\varepsilon_0 d)$;
binding energy $= 1.2 \times 10^6\,$J mol^{-1}.

Heat and kinetic theory

HK1 $\dfrac{20p_0T_0}{(4T_0 + T)^2}$.

HK2   (a) $(p + ax^2/V_m^2)(V_m - xb) = xRT$;
(b) $0.15\,\text{K}$ too high.

HK3 $1/210$.

HK4 $202\,°\text{C}$.

HK5 $2 \times 10^{-7}\,\text{m s}^{-1}$.

HK6 $99.85\,°\text{C}$.

HK7   (a) $30\,\text{K m}^{-1}$; (b) qualitative; (c) $(T/\text{K})^2 = 16 - 150x/\text{m}$, where $x = 0$ when $T = 4\,\text{K}$.

HK8 $120\,\text{A}$.

HK10 $22.0\,°\text{C}$.

HK11 $1.52 \times 10^5\,\text{J m}^{-3}$.

HK12 $3.5 \times 10^2\,\text{m s}^{-1}$; $6.4 \times 10^{-13}\,\text{m}$.

HK13 $n\langle c \rangle/4$ or $n\langle c \rangle/6$ depending on assumptions;
$\pi\langle c \rangle\rho\omega a^4/4$ or $\pi\langle c \rangle\rho\omega a^4/6$ depending on answer to first part.

HK14 $125\,\text{s}$.

HK15 10^{-6} N.

HK16 $\dfrac{2.8n}{A}(Em)^{1/2}$; 2.65×10^{-9}Pa.

HK17 (b) 1.2×10^{23};
(c) 3.1×10^{24}.

HK18 $0.48\,p$.

HK19 (a) $17T/15$; (b) $7V/10$.

HK20 (a) $220\,\mathrm{m\,s^{-1}}$; (b) 1.2×10^{12}; (d) 6×10^{-10} m.

HK21 (a) $F\tau/2m$; (b) $n^*e^2\tau/2m$; (c) $0.23(m/3kT)^{1/2}/nS^2$;
(d) $1.4 \times 10^{-3}\,\Omega^{-1}\,\mathrm{m}^{-1}$.

HK22 Pressure $\approx 1.0 \times 10^{-8}$ Pa;
distance between oxygen atoms $\approx 1.4 \times 10^{-4}$ m;
root-mean-square speed $\approx 1.8 \times 10^3\,\mathrm{m\,s^{-1}}$.

HK23 Total work done on gas $= 15.7$ J;
change in internal energy $= -75.5$ J.

HK24 $11\,\mathrm{kW}$; 38%.

HK25 $mgl/2Ap$.

HK26 $2.44 \times 10^6\,\mathrm{J\,kg^{-1}}$.

Electrostatics

ES1   (c) $E = \dfrac{Qa}{\pi\varepsilon_0 r^3}$; $\phi = \dfrac{Qa}{2\pi\varepsilon_0 r^2}$;

      (d) $E = \dfrac{Qa}{2\pi\varepsilon_0 r^3}$; $\phi = 0$;

       1.92×10^{-24} J.

ES2 $\phi_r = \dfrac{Q}{4\pi\varepsilon_0 r}$ if $r > a$; $\phi_r = \dfrac{Q}{8\pi\varepsilon_0 a^3}(3a^2 - r^2)$ if $r < a$.

ES3   1.23 m.

ES4   (a) $qa/2\pi\varepsilon_0(x^2 + a^2)^{3/2}$;
       (b) $-qa/2\pi(x^2 + a^2)^{3/2}$;
       (c) $(q^2/4\pi\varepsilon_0 a^2)(1/\sqrt{2} - 1/4)$;
       (d) $(q^2/8\pi\varepsilon_0 ma)(1/\sqrt{2} - 1/4)^{1/2}$.

ES5

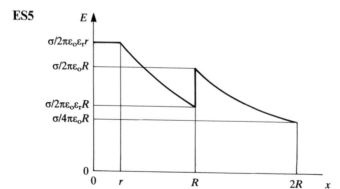

Fig. ES5.1

$V = -(\sigma/2\pi\varepsilon_0\varepsilon_r)\ln(R/r)$.

Answers

ES6 (a) $\delta Q/4\pi\varepsilon_0(R^2 + x^2)$, along the direction SP;
(b) $Qx/4\pi\varepsilon_0(R^2 + x^2)^{3/2}$, along the direction OP;
(c) $Q/4\pi\varepsilon_0(R^2 + x^2)^{1/2}$; maximum at $x = 0$.

ES7 (a) $V = q/4\pi\varepsilon_0(r^2 + x^2)^{1/2}$;
$E = qx/4\pi\varepsilon_0(r^2 + x^2)^{3/2}$;
(c) $E = q/2\pi\varepsilon_0 r^2[1 - x/(r^2 + x^2)^{1/2}]$.

ES9 $q(d - fx)/\varepsilon_0 A$; $\varepsilon_0 A/(d - fx)$.

ES10 11.8×10^{-12} F; 6.7 V; 32.8 V.

ES11 $\varepsilon_r\varepsilon_0 E_0^2/2$.

ES12 2.85 mm.

ES13 22 mm s^{-1} outwards.

ES14 (a) $\dfrac{Q^2 x}{2\varepsilon_0\varepsilon_r A}$; (b) $\dfrac{Q^2\Delta x}{2\varepsilon_0\varepsilon_r a}$;

(c) $\dfrac{\varepsilon_0\varepsilon_r E^2}{2}$; (d) $\dfrac{Q^2\Delta x}{2\varepsilon_0\varepsilon_r A}\left(1 - \dfrac{1}{\varepsilon_r}\right)$.

ES16 83.

Current electricity

E1 $L_c = 0.25\,\text{m}$; $L_m = 0.64\,\text{m}$.

E3 $R_1 = 112.5\,\Omega$; $R_2 = 11.25\,\Omega$; $R_3 = 1.25\,\Omega$.

E4 $R_x = 1800\,\Omega$; e.m.f. of cell $= 2.07\,\text{V}$;
internal resistance of voltmeter $= 1890\,\Omega$.

E5 $6.2 \times 10^{-2}\,\text{mm}$.

E6   (a) $11.8\,\Omega$;   (b) $0.16\,\Omega$.

E7 $2.05 \times 10^{-7}\,\text{V}$.

E8 $\dfrac{\rho \delta r}{2\pi r^2}$; $95.5\,\Omega$; $1\,\text{K s}^{-1}$.

E9   (a) (iii) 0.05%;   (b) (i) $229\,\text{kV}$, (ii) 0.

E10   (a) $P_L = P - P^2 R/V^2$;
(b) 99.5%.

E11 $32.1\,\mu\text{F}$.

E12   (b)

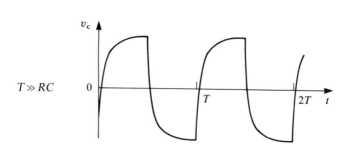

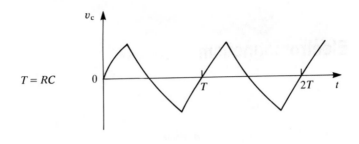

$T = RC$

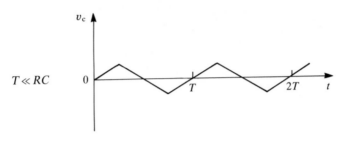

$T \ll RC$

Fig. E12.3

Minimum value of $RC = 0.025$ s.

E13 $R_A/R_B < 4$; $t = R_A C \ln 2$.

E14 $V_{out} = -\int V_{in}\, dt/RC$.

E15 (a) $-\pi/2$ (potential difference leads); (b) $\dfrac{R}{(R^2 + 1/\omega^2 C^2)^{1/2}}$.

E16 $3.6 \times 10^6\,\Omega$; $1.2 \times 10^{-3}\,$W.

E17 (a) 0.76 s.

E18 (a) $\sigma = j/E$; (b) $4.8 \times 10^{-14}\,$s;
(c) $1.2 \times 10^5\,\mathrm{m\,s^{-1}}$; $5.6 \times 10^{-9}\,$m.

E19 (a) $1.3 \times 10^5\,$s; (b) $1.2 \times 10^{-8}\,$m; (c) $1.7 \times 10^{-9}\,$s.

Electromagnetism

EM1

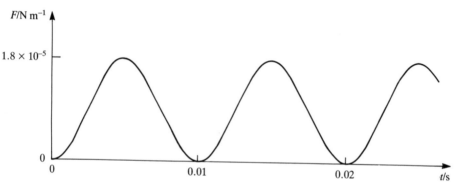

Fig. EM1.1

EM2 Net force on rectangular loop $= 8.0 \times 10^{-8}$ N in the horizontal plane, towards the straight wire;
induced e.m.f. $= 4.4 \times 10^{-6}$ V.

EM3 (a) $B = \mu_0 ID/2\pi y(D - y)$;
$\Phi = (\mu_0 IL/\pi)\ln(D - r)/r$;
(b) self-inductance per unit length $= (\mu_0 I/\pi)\ln(D - r)/r$.

EM4 Outside, $B = \dfrac{\mu_0 I}{2\pi r}$; inside, $B = \dfrac{\mu\mu_0 Ir}{2\pi a^2}$;

ratio of powers dissipated $= a/2x$.

EM5 4.65×10^{-12} T.

EM6 $BIl^2/16$.

EM7 $(R_m V/16a^2\rho)^{1/2}$.

EM8 $(10 \pm 1.7) \times 10^5$ Hz.

EM9 (a) 0.675 N; (b) 8.33 m s^{-1}.

EM10 2.1×10^{-4} m s^{-1}.

EM11 7×10^{-4} V.

EM12 $\pi a^2 nN\mu_0 I_0 \sin \omega t$; 0.

EM13 (i) Close S_2 for 0.07 s;
(ii) close S_1 and open S_2 quickly;
(iii) wait 0.035 s and open S_1.

EM14 (a) $I/A = 200\,t/s$;
(b) time constant = 0.003 s; final steady current = 0.6 A.

EM15 (a) $B = \mu_0 nI$; $L = \mu_0 n^2 \pi r^2 l$;
(b) $B^2/2\mu_0$; (c) $\mu_0 nrA/2\rho$.

EM16 0.93 s.

EM18 $\Delta x/x = -3.9 \times 10^{-3}$ (a reduction in the extension).

EM19 (a) $(\mu_0 N^2 A/l)\, dI/dt$;
(b) $\mu_0 N^2 A/l$;
(c) decrease of $\mu_0 AN^2 I^2 \delta l/2l^2$;
(d) $\mu_0 AN^2 I^2 \delta l/l^2$;
(e) 10 A.

EM20 1.6×10^{-4} V.

EM21 2.7×10^{-6} m (peak).

EM22 270 V r.m.s.

EM23 $(R_p/R_s)^{1/2}$.

EM24 5.1×10^7 m s^{-1}.

EM26 $f^2 x^2/2V$.

EM27   (a) 2×10^{-5} s later;
        (b) 1.3 cm horizontal displacement.

EM28 $Y^2 = (eLB^2D/mE)X$;
        E about 4×10^5 V m^{-1}; B about 0.1 T.

EM29   (b) $r = 7.1 \times 10^{-2}$ m; $t = 3.0 \times 10^{-8}$ s; $p = 0.78$ m;
        (c) 9.0 m.

EM30   (a) Charge carriers are positive; $n = 4.0 \times 10^{19}$ m^{-3}.

Atomic and nuclear physics

A1 (a) 9.4×10^{16} electrons per second; (b) about 150 W;
(c) the minimum X-ray wavelength $= 1.24 \times 10^{-10}$ m.

A2 (a) 1.9×10^4 V; (b) 2.70×10^{-15} J;
(c) 7.3×10^{-11} m; (d) 2.67×10^{-15} J.

A3 $E = -\dfrac{me^4}{8\varepsilon_0^2 h^2}; \quad \Delta E = \dfrac{3me^4}{32\varepsilon_0^2 h^2}.$

A4 $\dfrac{n^2 h^2}{8L^2 m}$; yellow-green.

A5 (b) $n^2 h^2 / 4\pi^2 m d^2$ (n is an integer);
(c) 6×10^{-20} J; 2.4×10^{-19} J; 5.4×10^{-19} J.

A6 (a) 1.7×10^{-10} m;
(b) (i) 7.6×10^{15} s^{-1}; (ii) -6.8×10^{-19} J;
(c) 1.2×10^{-10} s.

A7 1.53×10^{-15} J.

A8 2.2×10^{-12} m.

A9 (a) $25/16$; (b) 4.

A10 (a) $u_0 p = u_m d$;
(c) $N x \pi d^2 (E - V)/E$.

A11 3.75 V.

A12 (a) $v_{\mathrm{m}} = [(2/m_{\mathrm{e}})(hc/\lambda - e\phi)]^{1/2}$;
(b) $(2m_{\mathrm{e}}y^2/eV)^{1/2}$;
(c) $r = v_{\mathrm{m}}(2m_{\mathrm{e}}y^2/eV)^{1/2}$;
(d) 10 mm.

A13 (a)

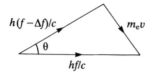

Fig. A13.2

(b) $m_{\mathrm{e}}v \approx [(2h^2f/c^2)(f - \Delta f)(1 - \cos\theta)]^{1/2}$;
(c) $h\Delta f = m_{\mathrm{e}}v^2/2$;
(e)

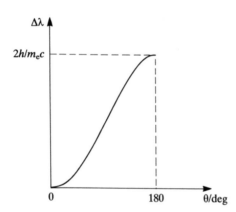

Fig. A13.3

A14 0.51 MeV; 2.4×10^{-12} m.

A15 $4.4 \times 10^7\,\mathrm{m\,s^{-1}}$.

A16 $6.72 \times 10^{-13}\,\mathrm{J}\,(4.16\,\mathrm{MeV})$.

A17 9050 years.

A18 The first scheme is not energetically possible, but the second is likely; age of earth $= 6 \times 10^9$ years.

A19 ^{238}U decay, 8α and $6\beta^-$;
^{235}U decay, 7α and $4\beta^-$.

Answers

A20 8.7×10^{-13} kg; 7.9×10^4 s.

A21 4×10^{-3}%.

A22 $0.05 \, \text{mm s}^{-1}$; 1.55×10^{17}.

Guidance

General physics, physical quantities and measurement techniques

G1 Either dimensions (M, L, T, etc.) or SI base units (kg, m, s, etc.) are acceptable for dimensional analysis. Remember that equations that are dimensionally correct are not necessarily physically correct.

G2 (a) If you are used to working with dimensions, you will be familiar with the notation M, L, T and Q for the dimensions of mass, length time and charge, respectively. You may prefer to work in terms of SI base units, in which case you will use kg, m, s and A (note: ampere rather than coulomb).

Tabulate the dimensions or base units of the quantities involved:

	Dimensions				Base units			
	M	L	T	Q	kg	m	s	A
e	0	0	0	1	0	0	1	1
ε_0	-1	-3	2	2	-1	-3	4	2
h	1	2	-1	0	1	2	-1	0
m	1	0	0	0	1	0	0	0
R	0	1	0	0	0	1	0	0

Put $R = ke^{\alpha}\varepsilon_0^{\beta}h^{\gamma}m^{\delta}$, and form an equation for each dimension or unit:

$0 = -\beta + \gamma + \delta$
$1 = -3\beta + 2\gamma$
$0 = 2\beta - \gamma$ (or $0 = \alpha + 4\beta - \gamma$ for the base unit method)
$0 = \alpha + 2\beta$.

The solution of the four equations is easiest in the order $\beta = -\alpha/2$; $\gamma = -\alpha$; whence $\alpha = -2, \beta = 1, \gamma = 2$ and $\delta = -1$. So

$$R = (k\varepsilon_0 h^2)/(me^2).$$

Substitution of values for the fundamental constants gives $R = 1.7 \times 10^{-10}$ m when $k = 1$. This is very close to the correct value of 5.3×10^{-11} m (the Bohr radius of the hydrogen atom); the Bohr theory shows that $k = 1/\pi$.

(b) If you try to set up an equation of the form $F = kR^\alpha \rho^\beta \eta^\gamma v^\delta$ and solve by the method of dimensions, you will find that you have only three simultaneous equations to find four unknowns, and the problem is insoluble. You should be able to identify two dimensionless groups of quantities by inspection: the conventional ones are $(vR\eta)/\rho$ and $F/(\rho v^2 R^2)$. In hydrodynamics theory, the quantity $(2vR\eta)/\rho$ is called *Reynolds number* and $F/(\rho v^2 R^2)$ is the *drag coefficient*.

G3 The intensity of the wave is the energy crossing unit area normal to the direction of propagation per second (SI unit: $\mathrm{W\,m^{-2}}$). Show that the resultant of the units on the right-hand side of the equation is also $\mathrm{W\,m^{-2}}$.

G4 The dimensions (or units) of a and b must be such that the quantities $(a\lambda/2\pi)$ and $(2\pi b/\rho\lambda)$ both have the dimensions (or unit) of (velocity)^2.

The change in b can be found by substituting into the given expression the data for each of the two temperatures. Subtract the two equations to find the value of Δb.

G5 The exposure time is easily found by application of the relation $\theta = \omega t$. Find the uncertainty in the exposure either by the addition of the fractional uncertainties in θ and ω, or by the substitution of extreme values in the original relation.

G6 The components of the velocity are given by differentiation of the components of the displacement:

$$\mathrm{d}x/\mathrm{d}t = \omega a \cos \omega t, \qquad \mathrm{d}y/\mathrm{d}t = -\omega a \sin \omega t, \qquad \mathrm{d}z/\mathrm{d}t = b.$$

The square of the magnitude of the velocity is obtained by taking the sum of the squares of the three components.

Similarly, obtain the components of the acceleration by differentiating the components of the velocity:

$$\mathrm{d}^2x/\mathrm{d}t^2 = -\omega^2 a \sin \omega t, \qquad \mathrm{d}^2y/\mathrm{d}t^2 = -\omega^2 a \cos \omega t, \qquad \mathrm{d}^2z/\mathrm{d}t^2 = 0.$$

The square of the magnitude of the acceleration is obtained by taking the sum of the squares of the three components.

The angle between the velocity and acceleration vectors is obtained by taking the scalar product between them: for two vectors $\mathbf{A}$ and $\mathbf{B}$ at an angle θ, $\mathbf{A} \cdot \mathbf{B} = AB \cos \theta$. The scalar product of the velocity and acceleration vectors $\mathbf{v}$ and $\mathbf{a}$ is $(v_x a_x + v_y a_y + v_z a_z)$. Show that this is equal to zero, i.e. that $\theta = 90°$ $(\cos \theta = 0)$.

G7 The diagram (Fig. G7.1) shows the coordinates of the two masses on the *x*-axis.

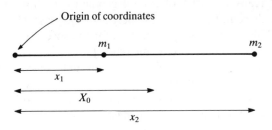

Fig. G7.1

If the centre of mass is at X_0, then taking moments about the origin:

$$m_1 x_1 + m_2 x_2 = (m_1 + m_2) X_0.$$

Rearrange this to find the expression for X_0.

For a system of particles in a plane, the coordinates X_0 and Y_0 of the centre of mass are determined separately, by taking moments first about the *y* axis and then about the *x* axis. Applying this idea to the particles A, B and C (of equal mass), we have $X_0 = (x_1 + x_2 + x_3)/3$ and $Y_0 = (y_1 + y_2 + y_3)/3$. The coordinates of the centre of mass are thus:

Time	X_0	Y_0
0	2	2
later	4/3	4/3
later still	1	1

By inspection, or by drawing a graph, all these points lie on the line $y = x$, and this must be the line of action of the external force. Because the centre of mass is moving from the point $(2, 2)$ towards the origin, the force must be directed from the positive quadrant towards O.

G8 Suppose the car is a distance L from the gate when the warning is given. The car can stop safely if $L > v^2/2a$ and pass safely if $L < vT$.

However, if $v^2/2a > vT$, there will be a range of values of L for which the car neither stop nor cross. Hence the value of v_{max}.

It is instructive to show these conditions on graphs of L against v.

G9 Remember to work in consistent SI units. The answers emphasise the value of petrol as a store of useful work.

G10 (a) If the surfaces are rough the inner sphere can only move by rolling. It is really a matter of careful geometry to show that, as the sphere rolls round the bowl, the height of the mass M remains unaltered. [This is obvious by inspection for the special case where the sphere has rolled half its circumference.]

Since the potential energy of M remains unchanged and the potential energy of the sphere must increase when it is displaced slightly from its equilibrium position, the system is stable for all values of M and for a sphere of any mass.

(b) Derive an expression for the amplification of a simple amplifier when part of the output signal is fed back to the input. Show that the system is always stable if the loop gain is less than 1.

Can the system ever be stable for a loop gain greater than 1?

G11 By conservation of angular momentum, the answer to (a) must be zero. For parts (b) and (c), since the change in radius is small, a differential approach is recommended. From the information given on moment of inertia, $I = kr^2$, so $dI = 2kr\,dr$ or $dI/I = 2dr/r$.

Apply the same idea to the equations $I\omega = $ constant and kinetic energy $= I\omega^2/2$, taking care over signs.

Energy has been fed into the system but the rotational kinetic energy has fallen. Where has the extra energy gone and how has it been used?

G12 The equation given will produce a straight-line graph if $\ln(n/\mathrm{m}^{-3})$ is plotted against $(T/K)^{-1}$: E can be deduced from the slope.

Consider carefully whether the shape of the graph supports the model over the whole temperature range.

G13 This question is an exercise in the analysis of numerical data, showing how one can proceed from a rough estimate to a more accurate value.

The graph of γ against E (Fig. G13.1) shows that the threshold photon energy, and hence the work function, is about 4.2 eV. Note the difficulty of obtaining an accurate value of E_0 from this graph: the curve approaches the E axis almost asymptotically.

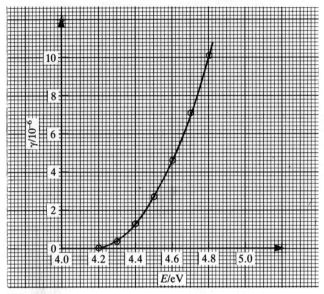

Fig. G13.1

If $\gamma = A(E - E_0)^n$, $\lg\gamma = \lg A + n\lg(E - E_0)$; thus a graph of $\lg\gamma$ against $\lg(E - E_0)$ will have slope n.

$(E - E_0)$/eV	0.1	0.2	0.3	0.4	0.5	0.6
$\lg[(E - E_0)$/eV]	-1.0	-0.70	-0.53	-0.40	-0.30	-0.22
$\lg(\gamma/10^{-6})$	-0.429	0.102	0.432	0.668	0.854	1.005

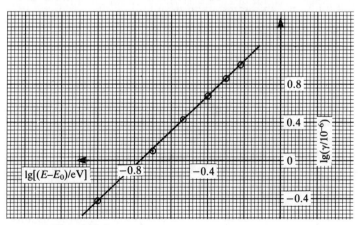

Fig. G13.2

The graph of $\ln\gamma$ against $\ln[(E-E_0)/\text{eV}]$ is a straight line, with gradient 1.85 (see Fig. G13.2); hence n, which must be integral, is 2.

Now if $\gamma = A(E-E_0)^2$,
$$\gamma^{1/2}/A^{1/2} = E - E_0$$

and

$$E = (1/A^{1/2})\gamma^{1/2} + E_0.$$

Thus a graph of E/eV against $\gamma^{1/2}$ will have an intercept on the E axis of E_0 (See Fig. G13.3).

E/eV	4.2	4.3	4.4	4.5	4.6	4.7	4.8
$\gamma^{1/2}/10^{-3}$	0.09	0.61	1.13	1.64	2.16	2.67	3.18

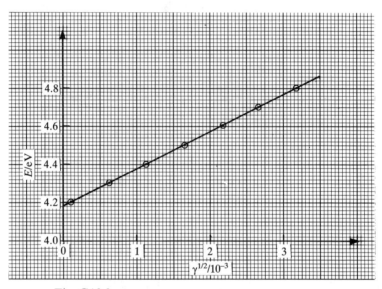

Fig. G13.3

From this graph, a more accurate value of E_0 is 4.18 eV.

G14 The first part of the question is designed to test the idea that distances, velocities and accelerations must be measured relative to reference axes.

The problem illustrates the effect of changing reference axes. It is fairly easy to decide what actually happens to the disc by considering its behaviour in the stationary frame. After it is released, since there are no forces acting on it, it will continue in a straight line with a linear velocity equal to that of the turntable at the point where it is placed. The linear speed at this point is $0.47\,\text{m s}^{-1}$ and the distance to the edge of the turntable is $1.32\,\text{m}$ measured along the chord.

To the observer on the turntable, the disc will not move in a straight line. Try to trace out the path it follows. When the disc leaves the turntable it will have a linear velocity, calculated above, and a tangential velocity due to rotation. These will add vectorially.

The observer on the turntable sees the disc change direction but is not aware of any forces on the disc. Therefore, he must either postulate that there are forces of which he is not aware or reject Newton's laws of motion!

Mechanics and gravitation

M1 (a) Since $P = Fv$, rewrite the equation as

$$F = P/v = Av^2 + B.$$

A graph of P/v against v^2 should thus be a straight line of slope A and intercept B. From the table in the question, calculate values of P/v and v^2.

$(P/v)/\mathrm{N}$	4.3	5.9	7.9	12.6	17.5	22.9	26.6	30.8
$v^2/\mathrm{m}^2\,\mathrm{s}^{-2}$	2.0	10.2	22.1	42.3	72.3	96.0	125.4	146.4

The graph (Fig. M1.1) is linear, has a slope of $0.19\,\mathrm{N}\,\mathrm{m}^{-2}\,\mathrm{s}^2$ and an intercept of $3.9\,\mathrm{N}$.

(b) Using $P = Fv$ again, express this as $F = P/(v^2)^{1/2}$; plot a graph of F against v^2 for the particular value of P of $60\,\mathrm{W}$.

$v^2/\mathrm{m}^2\,\mathrm{s}^{-2}$	10	20	30	40	50
F/N	19.0	13.4	11.0	9.5	8.5

The point of intersection with the line $F = Av^2 + B$ occurs at a value of v^2 of $34\,\mathrm{m}^2\,\mathrm{s}^{-2}$, corresponding to a speed of $5.8\,\mathrm{m}\,\mathrm{s}^{-1}$ (see Fig. M1.1).

Physically, the point of intersection of the straight line and the curve represents the values of v^2 and F for which the driving force provided by the cyclist is equal to the force resisting motion. This is the condition for the maximum uniform speed that the cyclist can sustain.

(c) The Av^2 term represents air resistance (see also question M9 for an analysis of why this force varies as v^2) and the B term represents friction in the mechanical parts (the bearings and chain) of the bicycle.

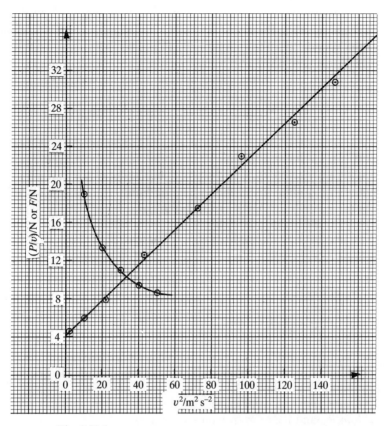

Fig. M1.1

M2 (a) The force is calculated directly from the defining equation for pressure. Assume that the area of the screen is about $0.1\,\text{m}^2$.

(b) The energy released as the atmosphere (pressure p_a) expands into the previously evacuated volume ΔV of the tube is $p_a \Delta V$. Assume that the volume of the tube is about $10\,\text{dm}^3$.

(c) Assume that all the energy of the implosion goes to the kinetic energy of the glass fragments. Take the mass of the glass as about $2\,\text{kg}$.

In this type of 'estimate' question, the answers should not be quoted to more than one significant figure.

M3 This is a fairly straightforward question. It does illustrate that you should think carefully about the choice of axes. Vertical and horizontal axes are not always the most convenient, and the first part of this question contains a strong hint on which axes to use.

Note that the acceleration of free fall is a vector and must be resolved into components along each of the new axes.

M4 The attractive force on the rocket by the Earth depends directly on the mass of the Earth and inversely on the square of the distance of the rocket from the centre of the Earth. As the rocket recedes, this attraction by the Earth reduces its speed, but the attractive force of the Moon is increasing, and eventually these opposing forces will be equal. You may find it helpful to sketch the attractive forces of the Earth and the Moon on the same axes for different positions of the rocket.

For the second part, it is difficult to apply the standard equations such as $v = u + at$ because the acceleration of the rocket is continuously changing. Use the principle of conservation of energy, remembering that, if the rocket left the Earth with just sufficient energy to reach the Moon, its velocity would be zero at the point where the resultant force changed sign, i.e. where the net attractive force first became directed towards the Moon.

M5 (a) For the orbit to be stable, $mv^2/R = GmM/R^2$, where R is the radius of the Earth.

(b) Consider whether the vehicle has zero kinetic energy (in space) before launch.

(c) Recall that the vehicle has both potential energy and kinetic energy. Try to work out the change in both of these quantities if the radius of the orbit decreased by a small amount δR. Pay special attention to the signs.

(d) As the vehicle approaches the Moon, it loses potential energy $GM_M m/R_M$ and hence must gain kinetic energy.

The original path of the vehicle may be found by conservation of angular momentum (originally mvX). A diagram will help (see Fig. M5.1).

(e) Work out the kinetic energy, and hence v_M, when the vehicle is closest to the Moon.

This shows that the velocity must be reduced from $2.5 \times 10^3 \, \mathrm{m\,s^{-1}}$ to $1.7 \times 10^3 \, \mathrm{m\,s^{-1}}$ and that the corresponding change in momentum is achieved by applying reverse thrust (i.e. a force) from the rocket motors for a certain time.

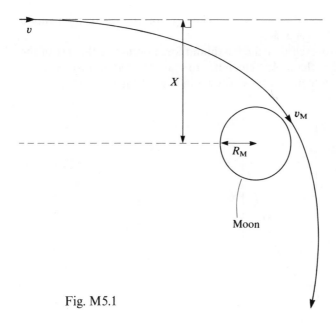

Fig. M5.1

M6 Use Newton's second law in the form 'force = rate of change of momentum' to find the thrust exerted by the rocket gases. The rate at which the gases are generated is $16\,\text{kg}\,\text{s}^{-1}$ and their velocity relative to the rocket is $2.5 \times 10^{3}\,\text{m}\,\text{s}^{-1}$: the thrust is thus $16 \times 25 \times 10^{3}\,\text{N}$. Note that the thrust is less than the initial weight of the rocket, so that it does not lift off immediately. The time interval between ignition and lift-off is calculated by finding the time taken for the weight of the rocket plus fuel to reduce to $4.00 \times 10^{4}\,\text{N}$, the thrust produced by the rocket motor.

M7 Show that the reduction in weight required for balance because some sand is in transit, rgt, is equal to the force on the pan when the momentum of the sand is destroyed upon reaching the pan. There are three separate stages that you should show on the graph: namely, the initial stage when the sand has started to fall from the bag but not yet reached the pan; the middle (steady-state) stage when there is a steady stream of falling sand; and, finally, the last stage when all the sand has left the bag but not yet reached the pan.

M8 The force on the table will be made up of that due to the chain already on the table, Mgl/L, plus the force due to the rate of change of momentum as the chain hits the table.

At time t, the chain will be travelling with speed gt and, since the mass per unit length of the chain is M/L, the rate at which the mass is hitting the table is Mgt/L. The rate of change of momentum (mass × velocity) is Mg^2t^2/L.

Satisfy yourself that the maximum force occurs as the last of the chain strikes the table (remember to consider *both* terms).

Your graph should be as shown in Fig. M8.1.

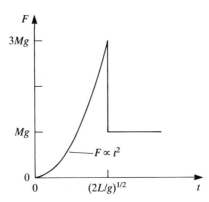

Fig. M8.1

M9 (a) (i) Find the force acting on the displaced liquid by using Newton's second law. Because the body is moving with uniform speed, there is no resultant force on it. Thus, the retarding force on the body is equal to the force that the body exerts on the displaced liquid.

(ii) In fact, not all of the displaced liquid attains the speed v, so that the momentum change per second is less than $Av^2\rho$ and the constant K is less than 1.

(b) (i) At the instant of release, a bubble is subject to two forces: the weight and the Archimedean upthrust. Because the upthrust is greater than the weight, the bubble accelerates upwards. As the speed v increases, so too does the retarding force (it varies as v^2). Eventually, the upthrust is balanced by the sum of the weight and the retarding force, so that the bubble moves with a constant terminal speed.

(ii) Write down the quantitative condition for the resultant force on the bubble to be zero. Note that, because the density of air is very much less than the density of water, the weight of the bubble can be neglected. The result is $K \approx 4rg/3v^2$.

(iii) Assume that the bubble remains at constant temperature, so that $pV = $ constant. Atmospheric pressure is equivalent to a head of about 10 m of water; thus, the fractional change in pressure in the bubble as it moves from the nozzle to the surface is $dp/p = -0.4/10$

(the minus sign shows that the pressure is getting less as the bubble rises). If the pressure gets less, the volume will increase; use the relation $dV/V = -dp/p$ to find the fractional change in volume. The fractional change in the radius, dr/r, can then be deduced: this works out at about 0.013. In (ii), you obtained the relation between the constant K, r and v: use this to show that the fractional change in the terminal speed dv/v is $(dr/r)/2$. The change of pressure thus makes a difference of only about 0.6% to the terminal speed.

You may also come across the case of a body moving through a liquid under streamline, rather than turbulent, conditions. In this case, the retarding force depends upon the viscosity η of the liquid, not on its density. Stokes' law states that the retarding force on a sphere of radius r moving through a liquid of viscosity η with velocity v under streamline conditions is given by $F = 6\pi r\eta v$.

M10 Conservation of energy, conservation of momentum and the identity $p = (2mE)^{1/2}$, obtained by combining $p = mv$ and $E = mv^2/2$, should give the first answer. Assume that the mass of the stationary nucleus is A times the neutron mass.

By differentiation (or inspection) of $E = E_0[(A-1)/(A+1)]^2$, E is a minimum when $A = 1$; hence, dense materials that are rich in hydrogen are best for shielding.

By writing down, in terms of E_1, the value of E_2 after a second collision, find a general expression for E_n. For a thermal neutron, $E_n = 3kT/2$, about 0.04 eV at room temperature. Since graphite is a form of carbon, $A_r = 12$.

In the final part, show that the speed of a thermal neutron is about $2.7 \times 10^3 \, \text{m s}^{-1}$, then substitute in $\lambda = h/mv$.

M11 Although the speed of the aircraft relative to the ground is the same whether it is flying due east or due west, the absolute speeds differ because of the Earth's rotation. Thus, the centripetal force experienced by the mass has different values, depending on the direction of flight. The reading on the spring balance is the gravitational force between the mass and the Earth *minus* the centripetal force acting on the mass. To obtain the absolute speed of the aircraft, you need to know the angular velocity of the Earth's rotation: remember that it makes one revolution in 24 h, so that $\omega = 7.3 \times 10^{-5} \, \text{rad s}^{-1}$.

M12 First draw a diagram showing the forces acting on the sphere when it is at the position P and the bowl is rotating with the critical speed. For an observer who is stationary outside the bowl, these forces are shown in Fig. M12.2.

The resultant of the reaction F (which is normal to the surface because the bowl is smooth) and the weight mg is the centripetal force. (What would be the force diagram for an observer rotating with the bowl?) Resolve the forces vertically and horizontally, and solve for ω.

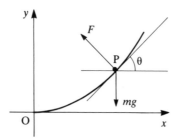

Fig. M12.2

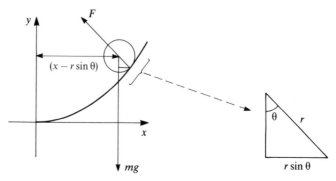

Fig. M12.3

If the sphere is larger than a point, the geometry becomes complicated. Draw a larger diagram, like Fig. M12.3, so that you can show that the radius of rotation of the sphere about the y axis is $(x - r \sin \theta)$.

Find the condition for the centripetal force to be the resultant of F and mg: this is

$$\omega^2 = (2ag)/[1 - 2ar/(1 + 4a^2x^2)^{1/2}].$$

The angular speed for dynamic equilibrium is no longer independent of x.

M13   The static friction is the resultant, obtained by vector addition, of the force needed to accelerate the mass tangentially and the centripetal force acting radially; it becomes limiting when the particle starts to slip. It is not necessary to know the value of this limiting frictional force. Note that neither the mass nor the coefficient of friction is given in the question. You only need to know they are both the same in each case.

Remember to convert the angular acceleration into a linear acceleration for deriving the tangential force.

[It is instructive to consider in which direction the particle moves when slip occurs, and to consider why slipping continues once it has started.]

M14 Intermediate answers are

$$\text{(a) } \pi r^2 \rho v^2, \qquad \text{(b) } \pi r^2 \rho v^2,$$
$$\text{(c) } \pi r^2 \rho v^3, \qquad \text{(d) } \pi r^2 \rho v^3/2.$$

Suggest reasons why answer (d) should be only half answer (c).

M15 (a) The stars rotate with equal angular velocities ω about their common centre of mass: ω may then be found by equating the inward mass × acceleration of either star to the gravitational force of attraction.

(b) Standard expressions for the total potential energy and total kinetic energy of the system can be combined if the value for ω^2 found in the first part of the question is substituted into the expression for kinetic energy.

(c) First calculate the Doppler shift due to the linear motion of the star system. Then find the effect of linear motion of the two stars when the line joining them is normal to the line of observation. Both ω and the period will have to be calculated.

M16 (a) The maximum power available will be the (total) kinetic energy of the wind destroyed per second. This may readily be obtained by first finding the volume of wind striking the sail per second (area × wind speed) and hence its mass.

Note that the maximum available power increases as (wind speed)^3.

(b) In this case, the maximum power is the potential energy destroyed per second. Note that (1) the centre of gravity of the water only moves 5 m in every 6 h period, and (2) an answer of 5×10^8 W could also be justified on the basis that no energy is available over the next 6 h while the water level is rising.

(c) In the final part of the question, first show that the total output to be stored is about 6×10^{13} J.

Next, a valid simplifying assumption is that the depth of the reservoir is small compared to its height and that the water is taken from a lake, the level of which remains constant.

Hence, show that the product of the area A of the reservoir, depth d and height h above the lake is about $6 \times 10^9 \, \text{m}^4$. Sensible values would be $h = 500 \, \text{m}$, $d = 60 \, \text{m}$ and $A = 2 \times 10^5 \, \text{m}^2$.

Additional comment—a nearby lake would be useful! If d is large, the reservoir will be expensive to build; if h is large, pumping will be a problem.

M17 This problem must be approached very logically to avoid confusion. Accordingly, a complete solution is provided.

When the body is at an arbitrary distance r from the centre of the circle, the *inward* force F on it is given by

$$F = k/r^n - mv^2/r.$$

If r increases to $(r + dr)$, the increase in the inward force is

$$dF = - nk \, dr/r^{n+1} - 2mv \, dv/r + mv^2 \, dr/r^2$$

(remember that both r and v will change).

By conservation of angular momentum, $mvr = \text{constant}$. Hence, $mv \, dr + mr \, dv = 0$ and $dv = - v \, dr/r$. The increase in the inward force dF thus becomes

$$dF = - nk \, dr/r^{n+1} + 2v^2m \, dr/r^2 + v^2m \, dr/r^2$$
$$= (- nk/r^{n+1} + 3mv^2/r^2) \, dr.$$

Now, if r is the equilibrium radius r_0, then

$$k/r_0^n = mv^2/r_0.$$

Hence, the increase in the inward force is now

$$(mv^2/r_0^2)(3 - n) \, dr.$$

The motion is stable if this is positive—an increase in radius is counteracted by increased inward force; otherwise, it is unstable, i.e. for stability, $(3 - n) > 0$.

M18 For this, and any, satellite in orbit, the gravitational attraction may be equated to the centripetal force; try to simplify your expression for the orbiting velocity to $(Rg)^{1/2}$, where R is the Earth's radius, before substituting numbers.

For the second part, remember that the satellite is to be launched from a surface that, because of the Earth's rotation, is moving. The satellite's launching velocity of $8000 \, \text{m s}^{-1}$ will be added (vectorially) to any velocity it *already* possesses because of the Earth's rotation.

[Hint: the period of the Earth's rotation on its own axis is more usually called a day!]

Note, finally, that only the Earth's rotation about its own axis needs to be considered. Motion of the Earth in its orbit round the Sun will affect the north pole and Cambridge equally.

M19 This problem is fairly typical of gravitational questions where the mass of a body cannot be assumed all to act at a point. It is more difficult than most at this level, so a detailed solution is given to illustrate the principles involved.

The force on a small mass m near the surface of this 'flat Earth' is mg—by definition. From the law of gravitation, the force is also GMm/d^2, where M is the total mass of the 'flat Earth'. Hence

$$mg = \frac{GMm}{d^2} \quad \text{or} \quad g = \frac{GM}{d^2}.$$

The problem now is that different parts of the 'flat Earth' are different distances from m, so d is different for different parts of the big mass M.

The disc is 'large', so it can be considered as extending to infinity, and the first step in the calculation is to divide the disc into thin slices, each δx thick (Fig. M19.1).

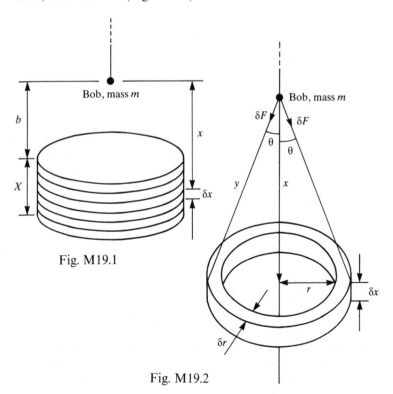

Fig. M19.1

Fig. M19.2

Now consider one slice, the midpoint of which is a distance x from m (Fig. M19.2). Within this slice, consider an annulus, radius r and thickness δr. This manipulation provides an annulus of the 'flat Earth' that is all approximately equidistant from m. Its volume is $2\pi r \delta r \delta x$, so its mass is $2\pi r \delta r \delta x \rho$. The force between this annulus and m is

$$\frac{Gm2\pi r \delta r \delta x \rho \cos \theta}{y^2}.$$

The $\cos \theta$ factor is included because force is a vector and the forces due to different short lengths of the annulus act as shown. All the horizontal components mutually cancel, but the vertical components ($\delta F \cos \theta$) all act downwards.

The total force due to all this slice can be obtained by integration. Note that there are two variables r and θ, but they are related because

$$r = x \tan \theta \qquad \text{so} \qquad dr = x \sec^2 \theta \, d\theta.$$

Express all variables in terms of θ and satisfy yourself that the correct limits for the integration are 0 and $\pi/2$. Thus the force on m due to the slice is

$$\int_0^{\pi/2} \frac{Gm2\pi(x \tan \theta)(x \sec^2 \theta \, d\theta)\delta x \rho \cos \theta}{x^2/\cos^2 \theta}$$

which simplifies to

$$\int_0^{\pi/2} 2\pi Gm\rho \delta x \sin \theta \, d\theta.$$

Remember that x is a constant for the one slice being considered, so the integral over the slice is simply $2\pi Gm\rho \delta x$. The force due to the whole slab is obtained by integrating over all slices, i.e.

$$\int_b^{b+X} 2\pi Gm\rho \, dx = 2\pi Gm\rho X.$$

Hence

$$mg = 2\pi Gm\rho X$$

and the thickness X can be deduced from g via the simple equation

$$g = 2\pi G\rho X.$$

M20 It is important to recognise the formal similarity to question M19. Once you have done so, the detailed advice given for that question should enable you to answer this one without too much difficulty.

M21 The first part can be solved by straightforward application of the laws of conservation of momentum and energy. However, since it is clear from the wording of the question that $M \gg m$, look for simplifying approximations such as

$$\frac{M+m}{m} \approx \frac{M}{m} \quad \text{or} \quad 1 + \frac{m}{M} \approx 1.$$

Some experience is required in knowing when to approximate. It must be done before the equations become impossibly complicated but, on the other hand, beware of writing

$$\frac{M+m}{M} \approx 1$$

in an expression such as

$$\left(\frac{M+m}{M}\right) - \left(\frac{2m}{\mu} + 1\right)$$

where simplification will show that the term m/M may be important.

For the last part, write down an equation for the rate of loss of kinetic energy in differential form, rearrange the variables and integrate (the integral is of the form $\int k\,dx/x^2$).

Note that, because it is losing energy, the big mass is slowing down. Accordingly, the rate of collision with gas molecules is decreasing and the deceleration of the body is changing with time. Thus, none of the standard equations requiring constant acceleration/deceleration can be applied, and the answer must be obtained by integration.

M22 The gravitational energy at a point is defined (by analogy with electrical potential) in terms of the work required to remove unit mass to infinity. Accordingly, the change in energy will be equal to the loss in gravitational potential energy when a shell of dust of mass $\delta m\,(= \rho 4\pi r^2 \delta r)$ condenses onto the sphere from infinity. Note that, for this part of the problem, r and δr are both constant. When the shell of dust is a distance x from the centre of the sphere, the attractive force is

$$F = \frac{Gm\delta m}{x^2}$$

and the mass m of the sphere acts as if it were all at the centre.

The work done on the mass δm is given as usual by $\int_{\infty}^{r}(-F)\,dx$, and the first part is completed by substituting for m and δm.

The last part should cause no problem once you have satisfied yourself about the first answer being correct.

M23 (a) This follows directly from applying $g = -dV/dr$ near the Earth's surface.

(b) Don't forget that, in a fixed orbit, the total energy of a satellite is the sum of its kinetic and potential energies. You should be able to show that $PE = -2 \times KE$.

A solution based solely on KE will give the right answer with the wrong sign.

(c) From the inverse square law, the gravitational field strength is proportional to $1/R^2$. Hence $dg/g = -2\,dR/R$, where dR is the height of Everest. What is the significance of the minus sign?

(d) The whole of the mass of the Earth may be assumed to act at its centre, but for $r < R_E$, the radius of the Earth, only the mass of the sphere of radius r contributes to the gravitational field strength at r. Hence

$$g_r = G\frac{4\pi r^3 \rho}{3r^2} = kr,$$

where k is a constant.

(e) For a typical mine shaft 1 km deep, $dg/g = -1/6400$ that is $= -1.5 \times 10^{-4}$. To test this change to 10%, a precision of 1.5 in 10^5 in the measurement of g would be required.

(f) Satisfy yourself that g is smaller above less massive oil-bearing rock. Now show that the observation follows from the fact that the water surface must be an equipotential surface.

M24 When both mass and velocity are changing, Newton's law that force equals rate of change of momentum becomes, in this context,

$$F = m\,dv/dt - v\,dm/dt + u\,dm/dt,$$

where v refers to the rocket and u to the fuel. This may be simplified to

$$F = m\,dv/dt - u^*dm/dt,$$

where u^* is the velocity of the fuel relative to the rocket.

In this problem, $F\,(=mg)$ is the downward force due to gravity. Hence

$$m\,dv/dt = u^*\,dm/dt - mg,$$

and the rocket can only take off if $u^*\,dm/dt > mg$: rearranging gives

$$dv/dt = u^*(dm/dt)/m - g.$$

This last expression shows that dv/dt is a maximum when m is least, i.e. at the end of burn-out.

The reason for multi-stage rockets should be apparent from this result.

M25   Since the gas remains at constant temperature, Boyle's law applies. If p_y is the pressure of the gas in the cylinder when the piston is at a distance y from the original position, $p_y = (p_0y_0)/(y_0 + y)$.

At this position, the piston experiences (i) a force acting to the left due to atmospheric pressure acting on the area A, (ii) a force acting to the right due to the pressure p_y of the gas inside the piston. The net force (due to the pressure difference) acting on the piston is thus $(p_0yA)/(y_0 + y)$, to the left; this is balanced by the force F to the right provided by the spring.

To find the work done by the gas in the expansion, integrate $F\,dy$ between the limits 0 and $2y_0$.

The force F in the spring when $y = 0$ is zero; find the value of F when $y = 2y_0$. Hence find Δy, the extension of the spring, in terms of p_0, A and k. The work done in stretching the spring is $k(\Delta y)^2/2$.

M26   (a) First form the analogue of Newton's second law of motion to relate ω to $d\omega/dt$. The integral form of this equation gives ω as a function of t.

(b) The graph is one of exponential decay of angular speed with time, with $\omega = \Omega$ at $t = 0$.

(c) To find the time at which $\omega = \Omega/2$, substitute this into the integral form of the equation in (a).

The area under the graph of angular speed against time gives the total angle turned through (just as the area under a graph of velocity against time gives the distance travelled). To deduce the number of revolutions made by the turntable, the area under the graph (between appropriate limits) should be found by integration of ω with respect to t.

Oscillations and waves, particularly light and sound

W1 Show that the relevant solid angle into which the lamp radiates is $\pi r^2/4\pi R^2$, where $r = 1.0$ cm and $R = 100$ m. When converting the energy falling on to the film into a number of photons, a fixed value of λ in the middle of the visible range may be assumed.

The focal length of the lens was given simply to establish the geometry. It does not enter the calculation.

W2 (a) Reflective properties determine colour, but only colours present in the beam can be reflected. Discuss the differences in the spectral distribution between artificial light sources and daylight, and indicate the reasons for these differences.

(b) Consider how the interference effect arises and hence show that the order of interference is high; thus, a long wave train (long coherence length, highly monochromatic beam) is required.

(c) The de Broglie relationship between the wavelength of an electron and its momentum is $\lambda = h/p$. Hence, show that for the electrons $\lambda = h/(2\,meV)^{1/2}$ and this value of λ is too small, relative to the slit width, for diffraction effects to be observed.

(d) By using simple vector diagrams and, where necessary, resolving the electric vector in two directions at right angles, explain why light is transmitted at certain angles.

The frequency of $4f$ arises because there are four positions of zero transmission during a $360°$ rotation.

W3 You should be familiar with vectorial addition of velocities. The second part of this question requires vectorial addition of accelerations. It is important to realise that the motion takes the same form as that of a simple pendulum in the laboratory. The equilibrium position of the pendulum is still along the line of the resultant acceleration.

The last part should cause no difficulty provided you resolve the forces and mass × acceleration carefully. Since the instantaneous acceleration of the mass is at right angles to the string, it is better to resolve along the string and at right angles to it rather than vertically and horizontally. The most common error is to write $T \cos \theta = mg$.

W4   The last part requires careful thought. You should try to explain why and, if possible, how the period, the centre of oscillation and the amplitude all change.

W5   This is a fairly straightforward question, even though the physical situation may be new to you.

For the first part, show that the instantaneous kinetic energy is $(mA^2\omega^2 \sin^2 \omega t)/2$ and then recall that the time-averaged value of $\sin^2 \omega t$ is $1/2$.

For the second part resolve forces and mass × acceleration horizontally. Note that, if the springs make an angle θ to the horizontal, $\cos \theta = x/L$.

You should be able to show that

$$\ddot{x} = -(2T/mL)x.$$

The next two parts simply require substitution of data into equations that have already been derived, or are given, but it is of interest to comment on the magnitude of the values obtained. For example, the detectable kinetic energy is slightly greater than that due to random molecular bombardment. Is this an example of evolutionary optimisation?

W6   (a) First, form the equation of motion by applying Newton's second law, and show that the motion of the pan is simple harmonic with $\omega^2 = g/\alpha M$.

The displacement is zero at $t = 0$, so the reading at time t is $M(1 - \cos \omega t)$. The maximum reading occurs when $\cos \omega t = -1$ and is $2M$. $\cos \omega t$ is first equal to -1 when $t = \pi(\alpha M/g)^{1/2}$.

(b) Consider an object of mass M_0 held in contact with the pan with $x = 0$ and released at $t = 0$. As the object and pan move downwards, the reading of the machine increases from 0 through M_0 to a maximum value, which we have to find. For readings from 0 to fractionally below M_0, the motion is the first quarter of a simple harmonic cycle with $\omega_1^2 = g/\alpha_1 M_0$. The amplitude of this part of the motion is $\alpha_1 M_0$, so the speed v of the pan as the reading passes through M_0 is $M_0\omega_1\alpha_1$. There is no sudden change in speed as the object passes through this equilibrium position. However, when the readings exceed M_0, the motion is again part of a simple harmonic cycle but, this time, it is characterised by $\omega_2^2 = g/\alpha_2 M_0$. The amplitude of this part of the motion is $v/\omega_2 = M_0\omega_1\alpha_1/\omega_2$. The graph (Fig. W6.2) shows how the displacement x varies with time t.

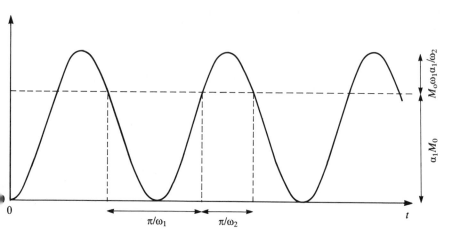

Fig. W6.2

The time for one complete oscillation is equal to half a period of the oscillation of angular frequency ω_1 plus half a period of the oscillation of angular frequency ω_2, i.e.

$$\pi[(1/\omega_1) + (1/\omega_2)] = \pi(M_0/g)^{1/2}[\alpha_1^{1/2} + \alpha_2^{1/2}].$$

The maximum displacement is given by the sum of the two amplitudes, i.e.

$$M_0\alpha_1 + M_0(\alpha_1\alpha_2)^{1/2}.$$

This corresponds to a mass reading of

$$M_0[1 + (\alpha_1/\alpha_2)^{1/2}].$$

W7 The first two parts are fairly straightforward. Define, carefully, the positive direction of x (the distance of the mass from O) or you will have difficulty with signs. In the second part, the motion is simple harmonic with the same period about a point

$$\frac{mg \sin \alpha}{k} \text{ below O.}$$

It is useful to recall that, if a constant c is added to x to form a new variable, i.e. $x_1 = x + c$, differentiation with respect to time shows that $\dot{x}_1 = \dot{x}$ because $\dot{c} = 0$.

In the last part, you should be able to show that the body does not move at all if

$$x < \frac{mg}{k}(\mu \cos \alpha - \sin \alpha).$$

If

$$x > \frac{mg}{k}(\mu \cos \alpha - \sin \alpha),$$

there is a new origin at

$$\frac{mg}{k}(\sin \alpha - \mu \cos \alpha) \text{ below O}$$

and the body comes to rest at

$$x + \frac{2mg}{k}(\sin \alpha - \mu \cos \alpha) \text{ below O.}$$

You can now calculate a new condition that the body will remain at rest.

Note that, in this situation, the motion is *never* simple harmonic. The frictional force is numerically constant, like the gravitational force down the plane, but it changes direction each half-cycle. To appreciate the difference, write down the equations for motion with friction on a horizontal surface and show that they *cannot* be worked into the same form as in the second part of this question.

W8 This is a difficult idea to handle properly the first time you meet it. The following approach is suggested. If the two masses and the light spring are considered as a 'system', there is no *external* force acting on the system (the only force on m_2 is that due to m_1 and vice versa). Therefore, the centre of mass of the system (see Fig. W8.1) does not move during the vibration. In other words, m_1 *behaves* as if it were a mass vibrating on the end of a spring of length $m_2l/(m_1 + m_2)$ attached to a *fixed* support (see Fig. W8.2). Furthermore, if a force μ causes unit extension of a spring of length l, a bigger force $\mu(m_1 + m_2)/m_2$ will be required to cause the same extension in a shorter spring of length $m_2l/m_1 + m_2$). At equilibrium, the extension is ε, where

$$m_1 g = \varepsilon \frac{(m_1 + m_2)}{m_2}\mu. \tag{1}$$

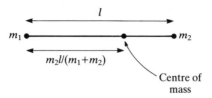

Fig. W8.1

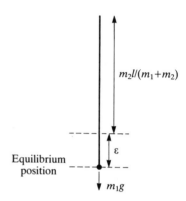

Fig. W8.2

If the mass m_1 is pulled down a further distance x, the downward force is $m_1 g$ and the restoring force is

$$(\varepsilon + x)\left(\frac{m_1 + m_2}{m_2}\right)\mu.$$

Hence

$$m_1 g - (\varepsilon + x)\left(\frac{m_1 + m_2}{m_2}\right)\mu = m_1 \ddot{x}.$$

Substituting for ε from equation (1) and simplifying gives

$$\ddot{x} = -\mu\frac{(m_1 + m_2)}{m_1 m_2}x,$$

from which it follows that

$$T = 2\pi\left(\frac{m_1 m_2}{\mu(m_1 + m_2)}\right)^{1/2}.$$

The remainder of the question is largely numerical substitution. Remember that one mole of atomic hydrogen has a mass of 1.0 g, *not* 1.0 kg.

W9 Remember that

$$n_3 \sin \theta = n_1 \sin r$$

at the first refraction, and a similar equation can be used to summarise the critical condition that light should just suffer total internal reflection at X (and at X′, etc.). Combine these equations, using the fact that, at the maximum value of θ, r will be equal to $(90° - C)$, where C is the critical angle for total internal reflection at X. You will find that the identity

$$\sin^2 \phi + \cos^2 \phi = 1,$$

for all ϕ, simplifies your equation to the required result.

Without cladding, surface scratches would invalidate the assumption of total loss-free internal reflection at X, X′, etc.

W10 If the last part causes difficulty, reconsider the problem of constructive interference from first principles. If $c = f\lambda$ and c changes because the wave has entered a medium of different refractive index but f remains constant, what happens to λ?

W11 The requirement in the question for you to draw a diagram is intended to help you to understand what is happening in the second part of the question. However, there is sufficient information here for you to put dimensions on your drawing using the standard equation for fringe separation, $x = \lambda D/2a$.

In the second part, the condition for destructive interference will determine the wavelengths absent from the light passing through the third narrow slit. Satisfy yourself that there will be a missing wavelength for every order of interference n. However, most values of n will give values of λ that are either greater than (n too small) or smaller than (n too large) the visible range of wavelengths. As indicated in the answer, there are only three values of n that correspond to values of λ that are within the visible range, i.e. $4.5 \times 10^{-7}\,\text{m} < \lambda < 7.5 \times 10^{-7}\,\text{m}$.

W12 Remember that (1) the screen records intensities, (2) intensity = (amplitude)^2, (3) amplitudes, not intensities, must be added vectorially. If you use a vector notation in which the amplitude from each slit is represented by vector length and the phase is represented by vector direction, this question should cause no problem.

W13 First, identify the path difference between rays 1 and 2 as AP – QB in Fig. W13.2.

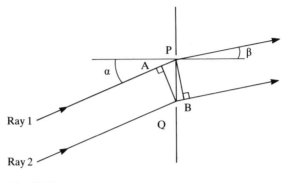

Fig. W13.2

The condition for maximum intensity in the emergent beam is that the path difference should be equal to an integral number of wavelengths of light.

Note that the X-ray scattering problem is analogous to that for light just dealt with. The equation is

$$4.2 \times 10^{-10} (\sin 30° - \sin \beta) = 1.4 \times 10^{-10} \, m.$$

Find the values of β that satisfy this equation for all the possible integral values of m. (You will find that $m = 0, \pm 1, +2, +3, +4$ are the only values for which $\sin \beta$ is between the values of $+1$ and -1.)

W14 The first part of this question is bookwork. You should try to draw carefully the effect of overlapping fringes. When slit S_0 is moved, calculate the point on the screen where the path lengths through S_1 and S_2 are equal. Remember that all angles are small. Explain carefully how this calculation relates to the distance moved by the fringe pattern.

In the final part, if the slit is widened in both directions from the centre, work out why the complete pattern is lost when the pattern from one edge is exactly out of phase with the pattern from the centre.

In the light of this calculation, what is the practical interpretation of 'narrow' in interference experiments?

W15 The answer can be obtained by two straightforward applications of the diffraction grating equation,

$$n\lambda = d \sin \theta.$$

Try, also, to solve the problem by differentiation, so that $\delta\lambda (= 6 \times 10^{-10}\,\text{m})$ can be substituted directly. If you choose the second method, only an approximate value for $\sin\theta$ is required.

W16 The most direct method of solution is to substitute the grating spacing $d\,(=10^{-3}/500\,\text{m})$ into the equation $n\lambda = d\sin\theta$ and calculate the values of θ corresponding to each order n of diffraction for the two wavelengths. Do not be tempted to use the small-angle approximation $\sin\theta \approx \theta$ to write $n\lambda = d\theta$ and $n\Delta\lambda = d\Delta\theta$. Although this will lead to the correct answer for the orders of diffraction that can be used, angles of $35°$ and $60°$ cannot be considered to be small.

W17 Clear diagrams help (see Figs W17.1 and W17.2). Consider why, despite the fact that there are three unknowns θ, s (the slit separation) and λ (the wavelength), the value of θ can be found from only two equations describing constructive interference.

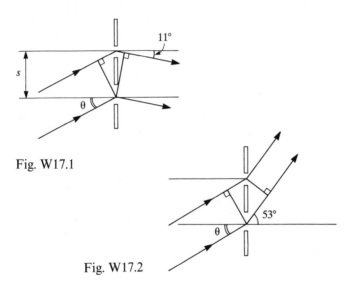

Fig. W17.1

Fig. W17.2

W18 (a) The two values of θ for the violet, blue and green lines in the range of values of θ between $30°$ and $50°$ are due to two different orders of diffraction (not necessarily the same orders for each colour).

From the grating equation $n\lambda = d\sin\theta$, try to find the order corresponding to each value of θ. For the violet lines, the ratio of values of $\sin\theta$ is $\sin 42.4°/\sin 32.7° = 0.6743/0.5402 = 5/4$. This suggests that the value of $42.4°$ corresponds to a fifth-order diffraction maximum, and the $32.7°$ value to a fourth-order maximum. Using these values of n, obtain two values of λ, $404.6\,\text{nm}$ and $405.2\,\text{nm}$, i.e. an average wavelength of $404.9\,\text{nm}$.

The values of θ for the blue lines also correspond to fifth- and fourth-order diffraction; for the green lines, the ratio of the $\sin\theta$ values is 4/3, corresponding to fourth- and third-order diffraction.

The values of θ for the yellow maxima are so close together that they must be due to two lines of nearly the same wavelength (a doublet) in the same order of diffraction. We know that the colour is yellow, and so expect the wavelength to be close to 600 nm. The only value of n that could give a wavelength in this region is 3. The wavelengths of the doublet should be regarded as distinct values and should not be averaged.

The largest possible value of $n\lambda$ is obtained by putting $\theta = 90°$ ($\sin\theta = 1$) in the grating equation. The maximum value of $n\lambda$ is thus 3.0×10^{-6} m. The closest approach to this is $n = 7$ with $\lambda = 404.9$ nm (violet), giving a value of θ of 70.9°.

(b) The advantage of using a spectrum at a large value of θ is that, at higher angles, the angular separation of the wavelengths is greater; that is, the *resolution* is better. However, when dealing with broad spectra, there is more overlap in the higher orders; also, the intensity of the lines is much less than that at lower orders.

W19 Referring to Fig. W19.1, the total path distance to the receiver is D. Waves are out of phase at the receiver at time t after switch-on, *but* waves were out of phase at the generators earlier than this, namely at time $t - D/c$ after switch-on, where c is the speed of sound. The

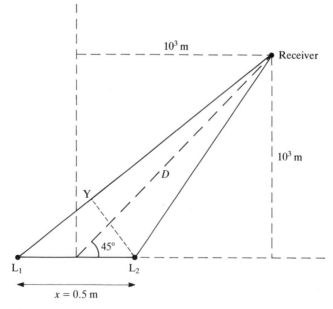

Fig. W19.1

frequency of emission, at this moment, was $10(t - D/c)$Hz. So the wavelength that causes interference is

$$\lambda = \frac{c}{f} = \frac{c}{10(t - D/c)}.$$

For the first silence, i.e. destructive interference, half this wavelength must be equal to the path difference (along the line to the receiver) at the loudspeaker, i.e. $\lambda \approx 2L_1Y$, where $L_1Y \approx x\cos 45°$.

W20 The first paragraph of the question is a piece of bookwork involving $p = h\rho g$, the answer being required for the second paragraph.

In the second paragraph, the meaning of the astronomical term 'occultation' is implied in the first sentence of the paragraph. Another consideration implicit in the question is that the cutting-off (or occultation) of the star's light is effectively instantaneous—the Moon has no atmosphere and, seen from the Earth, stars appear as point sources.

In the vacuum of space, the red and the blue of the star's light have the same speed (and travel the same distance). Accordingly, the time difference, Δt, occurs as the light passes through the Earth's atmosphere. The first paragraph of the question 'sets up' an atmosphere of uniform (optical) density, in which the product of refractive index and speed of propagation is constant for all colours. The question quotes only a very small difference in refractive index, so that, apart from the postulated uniform density, the *estimation* of Δt requires the speed of light in the atmosphere to have its *in vacuo* value. Using the relationship between time, distance (i.e. thickness of the atmosphere) and speed for the two colours leads, with only simple manipulation, to the answer.

W21 This is a question on interference of sound waves and the Doppler effect. You should try to provide a fairly detailed explanation as to why a straight-line trace appears on the screen in certain positions. You will need to think carefully about the addition of two vectors at right angles and their phase relationships.

Note also that the order of interference must be higher for the shorter wavelength.

W22 This question is a straightforward application of the Doppler effect formula for the case of a moving source and a stationary observer, $f' = f/(1 \pm v/c)$. The only complication is that there are *two* sources and f is the beat frequency between them; f' is the beat frequency as heard by the observer on the ground.

W23   This problem relates to the Doppler effect with electromagnetic waves. You can assume that, for relative speeds between source and observer that are small compared with the speed of light, the Doppler formula for sound, $f' = f/(1 \pm v/c)$, applies.

The stolen car, moving with speed v_c, and the police car, moving in the same direction with speed v_p, are equivalent to a suspect car moving with speed $(v_c - v_p)$ and a stationary police car. A radar wave *reflected* from the moving stolen car is equivalent to a wave emitted from a source moving with a speed $2(v_c - v_p)$. Apply the Doppler formula to show that the fractional change in frequency is given by

$$\Delta f / f = + 2(v_p - v_c)/c.$$

Since the fractional change is an increase, the police car is gaining on the suspect vehicle.

If the the radar unit is stationary, the magnitude of the fractional change in frequency is given by $2v_c/c$. This is likely to be a much larger change, because v_c is much greater than $(v_p - v_c)$, and so the method is intrinsically more accurate. Also, if the unit is mounted in a moving police car, it is essential to have an accurate knowledge of the speed of the police car at the instant of measurement.

W24   It is a little difficult to work out exactly what is happening in the situation posed by this question. First, you must appreciate that, when the Moon is directly overhead, the velocity of the transmitter and receiver on Earth due to the Earth's motion can be neglected because the transmitter and receiver are moving at right angles to the vector direction to the Moon. This gives the first answer, the speed of the spacecraft. Recall that the prefix giga (G) means 10^9 and remember that the velocity of the spacecraft will affect the apparent frequency of the signal both when the spacecraft acts as a receiver and again when it retransmits.

When the Moon is on the horizon at moonrise, the transmitter will have a velocity directly towards the Moon and this will affect the observations. Thus, the remainder of the question shows how astronomical observations may be used to give information both about the rotation of the Earth on its axis and also about its radius. Note that it is impossible to derive information about the absolute motion of a frame of reference in space (in this case the Earth) from observations made entirely within that frame.

W25   Since the chain is heavy and vertical, the tension in it will not be the same at all points. Hence, the speed of the wave will vary and the time of travel must be calculated for an infinitesimal portion, over which the speed can be assumed constant.

An integral of the form

$$\int kx^{-1/2}\,dx$$

is involved.

Take particular care with the signs in your integration or you will end with a negative time!

W26 A force acts on a wire carrying current in a magnetic field. The wire will move until the resolved component of the tension in the wire balances the electromagnetic force, so a good way to start the answer is to make a careful drawing showing all the forces on the wire at equilibrium.

The third paragraph, which requires a.c. theory, is not related to the second paragraph, where the current must be direct. If you are unable to solve this part, look up resonance, standing waves and, for the last line, Faraday's laws of induction. Electrical impedance is

$$\frac{\text{(applied p.d.)}}{\text{(current)}}$$

just as in other applications of a.c. theory.

Note that: (1) since the force is applied over a short distance near the centre of the wire, modes of motion in which the centre of the wire is a node are not likely, hence n is an odd integer only; (2) this wire also has a *mechanical* impedance defined as

$$\frac{\text{(applied force)}}{\text{(velocity)}}.$$

How does this vary near these frequencies?

W27 The frequencies that could be emitted by the 440 Hz string are 440 Hz, 880 Hz, 1320 Hz, ... The actual frequencies emitted depend on where the hammer strikes the string: because the 880 Hz string vibrates in sympathy with the 440 Hz string at a frequency of 880 Hz, the 440 Hz string must generate a substantial amount of energy in the 880 Hz mode.

The 220 Hz string could vibrate at frequencies of 220 Hz, 440 Hz, 660 Hz, 880 Hz, ...; however, it is driven by vibrations from the 440 Hz string, so the only frequencies actually emitted are 440 Hz, 880 Hz, ...

W28 (a) By inspection, the period of the modulation is 2 ms, hence f_s.

Again by inspection, E/E_0 is varying from 0.5 to 1.5. Accordingly, these are the minimum and maximum values of $(1 + m \sin 2\pi f_s t)$. Since $\sin 2\pi f_s t$ has minimum and maximum values of -1 and $+1$, respectively, $m = 0.5$.

(b) Clearly, one term is $E_0 \sin 2\pi f_c t$. Use the identity

$$\sin A \sin B = (1/2)[\cos(A - B) - \cos(A + B)]$$

to find the other two components. If this identity is unfamiliar to you, write down an expansion of $\cos(A - B)$, an expansion of $\cos(A + B)$ and subtract the two expressions.

(c) Recall that intensity is proportional to the square of the amplitude. For $m = 0.5$, the frequency spectrum will appear as in Fig. W28.2.

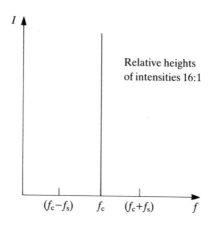

Fig. W28.2

Relative heights of intensities 16:1

(d) $f_c = 1$ MHz and $f_c = 10$ kHz, so the range is from 0.99 MHz to 1.01 MHz, i.e. the carrier occupies a band width of 20 kHz.

W29 For a particle of mass m, undergoing s.h.m. of amplitude A at an angular frequency ω, the energy of the motion is equal to the maximum kinetic energy of the particle, $m\omega^2 A^2/2$.

Now $\omega = 2\pi f$ and, for unit volume of gas, the total mass has the same magnitude as the density.

The intensity of a wave is a measure of the amount of energy crossing unit area perpendicular to the area of propagation per second. The value of I follows directly from this definition and the expression already obtained for D. (Imagine a cylinder of gas, of unit cross-sectional area and length v. All this gas passes a given point in one second.)

For the numerical part of the question, if the energy output is 10^{-3} W, the intensity at any distance R from the source is $10^{-3}/4\pi R^2$.

The rest is substitution. Sensible assumptions will have to be made for ρ (1.3 kg m^{-3}) and for v (330 m s^{-1}).

Note that A is of the order of one atomic diameter, so the ear is operating close to the limit of signal-to-noise set by Brownian motion.

States of matter

SM1   It is helpful to think of the mass supported by two wires, each of length $l/2$ and to let each wire extend by Δl. When the mass first comes to rest, energy conservation gives

$$mgh = 2(T/2)\Delta l,$$

where h is the vertical distance through which the mass has fallen and T is the tension in each wire. Use the Young modulus to eliminate T.

By applying Pythagoras' theorem to the triangle with sides $l/2$, h and $(l/2 + \Delta l)$, show that

$$h^2 = l\Delta l + \Delta l^2.$$

Hence justify

$$\Delta l \approx h^2/l,$$

and obtain an expression for h in terms of known quantities.

Note that you are *not* being asked about the equilibrium position. What further energy changes will occur before equilibrium is reached?

SM2   There is more than one way to solve this problem. One approach is to apply the idea of the first part of the question and convert the potential energy lost by the mass into stored elastic energy in the wire (see question SM1). Use this result, together with the standard equation relating stress, strain and the Young modulus, to calculate the maximum extension of the wire and hence the greatest tensile stress:

(maximum tension)
—————————————
(cross-sectional area) .

The minimum value of cross-sectional area that will ensure that this is less than the tensile strength can then be deduced.

SM3 Suppose the force constant of the rope is k and the rope extends a distance y when the climber is brought to rest. The loss in potential energy $mg(y + 2L)$ will be equal to the energy stored in the rope (force × extension/2). Also, as the climber is brought to rest, the net upward force will be $(ky - mg)$, and this must be less than $25mg$.

The particular rope breaks when the applied force is $25mg$ and the extension is $0.2L$: hence $k = 125\,mg/L$. Substitute this value in the energy equation and solve the quadratic in (y/L) to give a value of 0.187 which is just greater than 0.167 (1/6).

SM4 (a) If the student comes momentarily to rest after falling through the distance H, his kinetic energy was zero at the beginning and end of the motion: his total energy has changed only by the change in his gravitational potential energy. This energy goes into the work done in stretching the rope. Equate the decrease in the student's gravitational potential energy with the increase in the stored (strain) energy of the rope.

(b) It is easy to see that the motion is oscillatory: after the student reaches water level for the first time, the stretched rope will pull him up again. While the rope is in tension, the motion is simple harmonic, but, as soon as the rope becomes slack (which it must do, by conservation of energy), the student will be subject only to the constant acceleration of free fall. The graph of his velocity against time is thus a combination of uniformly accelerated motion under gravity (straight-line graphs, dashed in Fig. SM4.1 (p. 90) with positive gradient equal to g) and simple harmonic motion (parts of a sine curve). Note that the linear regions join smoothly to the sine curve segments.

SM5 Try to show that, in the general case when the volume can change, the fractional change in volume is

$$\frac{dV}{V} = \frac{dl}{l}(1 - 2\sigma),$$

where dl/l is the fractional change in length.

Substitute the experimental values of σ and suggest molecular mechanisms for the observed changes in volume when these different materials are stretched.

SM6 If the wire stretches but resistivity remains constant, the resistance of the wire will change. Show that the fractional change in resistance is

$$\frac{dR}{R} = \frac{dl}{l}(1 + 2\sigma),$$

where dl/l is the fractional change in length.

[Why is this expression different from the expression for dV/V in question SM5?]

Substituting approximate values will show that, for a change of $0.1\,\Omega$ in a wire $1\,m$ long, an extension of about $3\,mm$ and hence a force of $20\,N$ are required. A bigger change in resistance will require a bigger force, etc. Which combination of values do you think is most suitable, and how would you then make the measurements?

SM7 (a) Consider a section of the cable at a distance x below the point of suspension, and find the weight of the cable below this section; hence deduce the stress at the section. In drawing the graph, ignore any possible change in the cross-sectional area as a result of extension, and also assume that the extension of the cable under its own weight is very small compared with its length.

(b) In (a), you will have shown that the stress in a section of the cable at a distance x below the point of suspension is $(L-x)mg/LA$. The corresponding strain is $(L-x)mg/LAE$. Hence, find the strain energy stored in an element of length δx at a distance x below the point of suspension, and integrate this expression over the whole length L of the cable. An integral of the form $\int kx^2\,dx$ is involved, where k is a combination of constants.

(c) From the given expression for the strain energy, you can see that, for cables of the same length and area of cross-section, the strain energy is proportional to m^2/E, i.e. to ρ^2/E, where ρ is the density. Calculate values of ρ^2/E from the data in the question and put the metals into order of increasing strain energy.

SM8 The Avogadro constant is defined in terms of the mole. Also, the mole is defined in terms of the number of ^{12}C atoms contained in $12\,g$ (*not* $12\,kg$) of carbon-12. Given that the relative molecular mass of ice is 18, it follows that $1\,g$ of ice contains $(6 \times 10^{23})/18$ molecules. Each molecule has four nearest neighbours, but each bond is shared between two molecules. The total number of bonds is only $(4 \times 6 \times 10^{23})/(2 \times 18)$ and not $(4 \times 6 \times 10^{23})/18$.

SM9 If the graphs in the first part have been properly drawn and labelled (see any good physics textbook on this topic), parts (i) and (ii) should be straightforward. At equilibrium, there is no force on the atoms, $dU/dx = 0$. The dissociation energy removes an atom from equilibrium to infinity.

In part (iii), remember that, for two particles of equal mass, the vibration is symmetrical about their centre of mass for small amplitude. Write down the extra force when each mass is displaced a distance δx from equilibrium.

Expand the binomial to find the 'spring constant' and hence f from $(1/2\pi)(k/m)^{1/2}$.

M10 Think, first of all, why the centre of mass of the whole oscillating system must remain in the same position, whatever the mode of oscillation. (Remember that no external force is acting.)

Note that, in the first mode of oscillation, slider B remains stationary. The oscillations of sliders A and C are thus exactly the same as they would be if the springs were attached to a fixed point at B. The equation of motion of either A or C is simply

$$M(d^2x/dt^2) = -kx.$$

The frequency of this simple harmonic motion can be obtained directly.

In the second mode, the problem is more complicated. First, write down the condition for the centre of mass to remain stationary. If A and C are displaced distances y to the right of their equilibrium positions, and B a distance z to the left of its equilibrium position, then $mz = 2My$. Then consider the force acting on (say) C due to the extension of the spring: this is $k(y + z)$, to the left. The equation of motion of C is thus

$$M(d^2y/dt^2) = -k(y + z).$$

Substitute for z in this equation and obtain an equation of motion in terms of y. You should recognise this as simple harmonic motion of the required frequency. Equations of the same frequency would be obtained by considering the motion of sliders A or B.

In the last part, convert the wavelength of $3.9\,\mu m$ into a frequency of 7.7×10^{13} Hz. Substitute this into the equation for the frequency of mode 2 and obtain the value of k, which can then be used in the expression for the frequency of mode 1.

M11 You have probably had plenty of experience of discussing potential energy curves qualitatively. In this question, you are taken through a quantitative example, based on a situation that is probably more complicated than you have considered up to now. Parts (a) to (d) should be familiar ground.

(e) The total energy is made up of a proton–proton contribution and an electron–proton contribution. The proton–proton contribution can be calculated from the coulombic potential expression, with a proton–proton separation of 110 pm. The total energy at this separation can be read off from Fig. SM11.2, and the electron–proton contribution can be obtained by subtraction of the proton–proton contribution.

(f) For large values of r, the electron is likely to remain close to one of the protons, so that the system looks like a hydrogen atom plus a distant proton. Although the distant proton may have been taken almost to infinity, the total energy is not zero because the electron is still bound to the other proton, with a negative energy.

(g) From the answer to part (d), the energy required to separate *all* the particles to infinity is 2.6 aJ. You are told that the ionisation energy of a hydrogen atom (the energy required to remove an electron from the hydrogen atom) is 2.2 aJ; conversely, the energy released when an electron recombines with a proton to form a hydrogen atom is 2.2 aJ. Hence, the energy required to dissociate the singly ionised hydrogen molecule into a hydrogen atom and a proton is $(2.6 - 2.2)\,\text{aJ} = 0.4\,\text{aJ}$.

(h) The addition of a second electron to the system of Fig. SM11.1 will not affect the proton–proton repulsion energy but will increase the proton–electron attraction energy. Thus, the new graph of total energy against proton separation will show an equilibrium separation (a minimum) at a smaller value of r than before; the minimum of energy will be deeper than before; and at larger values of r, the new graph will be below that of Fig. SM11.2.

SM12   The description of the sodium chloride lattice in the question is perhaps the simplest one that relates to the cubic symmetry of the lattice, and you may like to satisfy yourself that each ion has six nearest neighbours of opposite charge by visualising eight such cubes packed to form a large cube (of side $2d$, where d is the distance between the centres of adjacent ions) as in Fig. SM12.1. It is not necessary to go as far as this to establish the effective volume of one NaCl formula unit. Because of the symmetry, the different sizes of the ions may be disregarded and any one ion may be regarded as uniquely occupying its own cube of side d, i.e. the centre of the ion being at the centre of such a cube. Two adjacent cubes then give the volume, $2d^3$, occupied by a single NaCl unit, and the rest follows.

Take care over the units in which you express the mass of one NaCl formula unit, i.e. remember that one mole of ^{12}C atoms has a mass of 12 g (0.012 kg) and that relative atomic masses are ratios and therefore dimensionless (see question SM8).

See also question SM13, which deals with the energy of ions in the sodium chloride lattice.

SM13   First, identify the six nearest-neighbour sodium ions, the twelve next-nearest-neighbour chloride ions, and the eight next-next-nearest-neighbour sodium ions. Work out the distance of each of these classes of ions from the central chloride ion P. Use the expression for the electrostatic potential in the field of a point charge to find the potential energy of P due to each of the remaining 26 ions in the crystal. You will find that the expression has alternate negative and positive terms, because the contribution to the potential from the positive sodium ions is negative and the contribution from the negative chloride ions is positive.

The binding energy of the crystal is the energy required to remove all the ions in it to infinity. For the section of the crystal shown in Fig. SM13.1, this could be obtained by calculating a term like V_{es} for each of the 27 ions in the crystal and adding up. For a crystal containing a mole of sodium chloride, there are l sodium ions and l chloride ions, $2l$ ions in all, where l is the magnitude of the Avogadro constant L, i.e. 6.0×10^{23}. To avoid counting each ion twice, however, a factor of $1/2$ is introduced, so that the binding energy is $2LV_{es}$.

Your answer is an over-estimate, as it is obtained by considering the contributions to V_{es} of the ions in only a limited volume of the crystal. To obtain a better estimate, one has to consider the contributions to V_{es} from the next-next-next-nearest neighbours, and so on. Unfortunately, the series of terms in the expression does not converge rapidly.

Even if the calculation were carried on until an acceptable degree of convergence had been obtained, it would be found that the calculated value for the binding energy was *greater* than the experimental value. This is because, apart from electrostatic forces, there are short-range repulsive forces in the lattice, which were neglected in the calculation of the potential energy. Whereas the electrostatic potential varies as $1/r$, these repulsive forces fall off much more rapidly, approximately as $1/r^9$.

SM14   Starting from stored energy = (force × extension)/2, which should be either proved or justified, the first part is straightforward.

(a) A qualitative answer in terms of the relative depths of the potential energy wells of atoms at the surface and atoms in the interior is the best approach here.

(b) For an area A of cross-section, $AZn_s/2$ bonds are broken and energy ε is required to break each bond. By noting that this creates a total area of new surface equal to $2A$, the answer follows.

(c) An estimate of the breaking stress may be obtained by assuming that, at breaking, the stored strain energy in the gap between the two layers of atoms must be sufficient to create the new surfaces. Hence, $\sigma^2 V/2E = 2A\gamma$, where $V = Ax$.

In real solids, dislocations, crystal slip planes and microcracks all cause local stress enhancement or 'weaknesses'. Impurities and the polycrystalline nature of material will provide some strengthening by trapping dislocations, but the structure will still be much weaker than this ideal model.

Heat and kinetic theory

HK1 The sensitivity can be obtained by differentiating an equation that relates the pressure p in the system to the temperature T of the bulb. This can be deduced by writing down the equation of state for an ideal gas three times, once for all n molecules of gas when the bulb and manometer are both at T_0, once for the n_1 molecules of gas in the bulb after the bulb has been heated, and once for the n_2 molecules of gas remaining in the manometer. The equation $n_1 + n_2 = n$ will then relate p and T.

   The last two parts show that, for an ideal thermometer, where there is no dead space, the sensitivity is independent of temperature but directly proportional to the mass of gas in the thermometer. The sensitivity is p_0/T_0 in (a) and $5p_0/4T_0$ in (b).

HK2 In the first part, the effect of x moles can be worked out by considering each term in turn. A neater solution is to realise that x moles occupying volume V are equivalent to 1 mole occupying volume V/x: the answer then falls out directly.

   For the numerical part, a differential method avoids heavy arithmetic.

   Given that the thermometer is at constant volume, that x is constant and that the equation of state is linear in p and T, differentiation shows that the actual behaviour is described by

$$\Delta p(V - bx) = xR\Delta T$$

(the symbol Δ is used here to show that changes are finite).

   The assumed (ideal) behaviour is given by

$$\Delta pV = xR\Delta T',$$

where ΔT and $\Delta T'$ are both approximately 100 K.

The above equations may be combined to give

$$R(\Delta T' - \Delta T) = b\Delta p,$$

where $(\Delta T' - \Delta T)$ is the (small) error in temperature.

Since $\Delta T' \approx \Delta T$, Δp can be substituted in this equation by

$$\Delta p = xR\Delta T/V.$$

Hence

$$(\Delta T' - \Delta T) = xb\Delta T/V.$$

Substituting $\Delta T = 100$ K, this being a sufficiently good approximation, leads to the answer.

HK3 This is a fairly straightforward question about method of mixtures. However, since the specific heat capacity of the silver is changing with temperature, the heat given out by the silver when it cools by a small amount δT at some intermediate temperature T must be worked out. The total heat given up by the silver sphere can then be obtained from an integral of the form

$$\int (\alpha T^3 + \beta T)\, dT.$$

HK4 This is a straightforward application of the thermal conductivity equation

$$dQ/dt = -\lambda A(d\theta/dt)$$

to two slabs of material in series. Form the two equations and eliminate the temperature θ at the interface between the shale and granite layers.

Geothermal energy can be extracted by pumping cold water down the pipe. At the bottom, the temperature is more than sufficient to convert the water to steam, which can be returned to the surface under pressure by another pipe and then used for heating or driving turbines.

HK5 This is a straightforward problem. The rate of flow of heat given by the conductivity equation can be related to the rate of increase of mass of ice via the specific latent heat of fusion. The rate of increase in mass of ice may be readily converted into a rate of increase of thickness of ice.

In the final part of the question, first note, from the equation already derived, that the rate of formation of ice decreases as the thickness of ice increases (the ice acts as its own insulator). In practice, the ice thickness will increase more slowly than the equation predicts because some of the heat will be used to cool the water from 4 °C to 0 °C. The interface must always remain at 0 °C.

HK6 In the steady state, the rate of energy conduction through the walls must be equal to the electrical power supplied. This principle may, in customary notation, be expressed as

$$kA(\theta - \theta_0)/x = V^2/R,$$

where θ denotes the oven temperature in the steady state, $\theta_0 = 20\,°C$ and V is equal to $10^7 \times$ thermo-e.m.f. at a temperature difference of $(100\,°C - \theta)$. Substituting all the numerical data now gives

$$45(\theta/°C - 20) = [400(100 - \theta/°C)]^2. \tag{1}$$

Satisfy yourself that θ would be expected to be of the order of 100 °C and then make use of this fact to simplify the above equation to

$$45 \times 80 = [400(\Delta\theta/°C)]^2,$$

where $\Delta\theta$ is the difference between the temperature of the steam and the oven temperature.

Note that the high-gain amplifier is behaving as a very effective oven thermostat and also that a four-significant-figure answer has emerged from two-significant-figure data! You might also like to satisfy yourself that rigorous solution of equation (1) also gives $t = 99.85\,°C$ and that the simplification is accordingly justified.

HK7 (a) This is a simple application of the conductivity equation.

(b) You should be able to convince yourself that the graph of temperature distribution will be convex upwards, above the $30\,K\,m^{-1}$ line, and may or may not show a maximum.

(c) The standard thermal conductivity equation has to be solved with the thermal conductivity λ set equal to kT, where k is a constant.

The integration is trivial as soon as the two variables have been clearly identified.

HK8 You will find it best to work in symbols, using $a(1 + b\theta)$ for the resistance per unit length of the copper strip. Consider the equilibrium of a piece of the strip that has length l and width w and equate the rate of production of heat within the copper from electrical power to the rate of loss of heat by conduction (in both directions) through the asbestos.

Hence show that

$$\theta = \left(\frac{2kw}{axI^2} - b\right)^{-1},$$

where x is the thickness of one asbestos sheet, I the current and k the thermal conductivity of asbestos. Deduce the value of I that allows θ to tend to infinity.

HK9 In the steady state, the rate of heat conduction across each small section of the tube is constant. Since the thermal conductivity is a variable, the standard equation can only be applied to a small length of tube, for example a length δl at a distance l from the hot end.

An equation relating the temperature at a point to the distance of that point from the hot end can then be obtained by integrating an expression of the form $\int kx^{1/2}\,dx$. Use the boundary conditions $T = 373\,\text{K}$ when $l = 0$ and $T = 273\,\text{K}$ when $l = L$ (the total length of the joining tube) to eliminate the unknown constants, including the constant of integration.

HK10 Since heat is conducted both ways from the centre, and the question makes it clear that the system is symmetrical about the midpoint of the rod, consider only half the rod. Note that, at a cross-sectional plane a distance l along the rod from the midpoint, all the heat generated between there and the centre, $I^2 Rl/2L$, must be transferred across this plane if the condition that heat is only lost from the ends of the rod is to be satisfied.

An integral of the form $\int kx\,dx$ must be evaluated to find the temperature difference between the centre of the rod and one end.

HK11 Combine the standard equation derived from the kinetic theory of gases, $p = Nm\langle c^2\rangle/3$, with an expression for the total kinetic energy of all the monatomic molecules in unit volume. Remember that monatomic molecules have only translational modes of motion, and that equipartition of energy may be assumed. The answer to the first part of the question then follows, as also does the conclusion that the kinetic energy per unit volume does not change with temperature provided the pressure remains constant. You can reach the same conclusion starting from kinetic energy $= 3NkT/2$, provided allowance is made for the fact that the number of atoms per unit volume will change.

Note that the gas would have rotational and vibrational contributions to its kinetic energy if it were not monatomic.

HK12 For advice on the first part, see question HK11. If you do not understand the next two parts, refer to question W23.

HK13 The Joule classification of velocities is normally acceptable at this level of application of the kinetic theory of gases. Quite by chance, the Joule classification does lead to the correct numerical factor $(1/3)$

in the formula for the pressure of a gas but it does not give the correct factor for the number of molecules striking unit area in unit time. The Joule classification gives $n\langle c\rangle/6$ whereas the correct expression is $n\langle c\rangle/4$. Try working out the correct expression by first considering those molecules in a hollow cone of angle between θ and $(\theta + \delta\theta)$ and then integrating over all values of θ from 0 to $\pi/2$ rad.

In the second part of the question, the molecules will strike both sides of the disc with random speeds c. When they leave the disc, they will have a systematic velocity v superimposed on c due to the motion of the disc. The momentum given to each molecule will cause a dragging effect on the disc. The drag on a molecule that strikes the disc between radii r and $r + \delta r$ is $m\omega r$ (hence drag increases with increasing radius). Remembering that there are two sides to the disc, the total number of molecules striking this annulus in unit time is

$$2 \times 2\pi r \delta r \times n\langle c\rangle/4.$$

The torque due to this annulus is the moment of this force about the centre of the disc, so the total torque involves an integral of the form $\int kx^3 \, dx$.

IK14 Use simple kinetic theory equations to estimate the number of oxygen molecules in the vacuum chamber (1.2×10^{11}) and their root-mean-square speed $(480\,\mathrm{m\,s^{-1}})$ (see also question HK22).

Using a very simple kinetic theory model, one can assume that one-sixth of the molecules in a gas are moving along each of the six coordinate directions. Thus, in a gas with n molecules per unit volume, each moving with speed c, about $nAc/6$ molecules will strike area A each second. Use this expression to find the number of oxygen molecules hitting the surface of the semiconductor sample each second, and hence find the time taken for the maximum acceptable surface concentration of oxygen molecules to build up. Question HK13 uses very similar principles.

IK15 Assume that the word 'random' implies that the motion is equivalent to two groups of 250 ants running at right angles to each other and parallel to the sides of the frame. Apply the ideas of the kinetic theory to this two-dimensional problem.

IK16 This question is designed to compare and contrast 'real' particles, i.e. those which have a mass even when at rest, and the particle-like properties of photons. For example, in each case the pressure can be expressed as the change in momentum per second on unit area but the expression $E = mv^2/2$, which can be used for the kinetic energy of the real particles, is not applicable to photons. What alternative expression can be used?

Note that the *maximum* change in momentum in each instance is when a particle is incident normally on the surface *and rebounds elastically*.

HK17 For the case of the pressure exerted by the 'photon gas', work through the simple kinetic theory derivation of pressure, remembering that the momentum change of a photon reflected normally from the wall is $2hf/c$ and that the time taken for the photon to traverse the container and come back to the wall is $2a/c$. To estimate the number of photons in the box, find the frequency of the light from $f = c/\lambda$ and substitute the values in the question.

To find the number N of gas molecules in the box, use the ideal gas equation in the form $pV = nRT$, where n is the number of moles of gas, and $N = nL$.

Sudden compression of the gas in the box, for example by pushing in a piston, will mean that the molecules rebounding from the piston have an increased speed; thus, the temperature of the gas increases. As a consequence of the increased speed, there is a bigger momentum change at each impact of a molecule with the wall and, moreover, impacts will occur more frequently; thus, the rate of change of momentum of the molecule, and hence the pressure, is increased.

If a similar kinetic theory argument were to be applied to the box containing the photons, you might expect the pressure due to the photons to increase. The frequency of a photon reflected from the moving reflecting wall will be changed; if you want to use the wave picture of light, your knowledge of the Doppler effect would lead to the same conclusion.

HK18 For an ideal gas, the equation $pV = nm\langle c^2 \rangle /3$ is always applicable In this problem, the volume V of each compartment is constant and the mass m of each molecule is also constant. Since $\langle c^2 \rangle \propto T$, the equation in the first line can be rewritten as $p = bnT$, where b is a constant that need not be further defined.

In the original condition, both compartments were at the same temperature and pressure and contained an equal number of molecules, n say.

On heating one compartment, the numbers of molecules on either side of the hole will change until the steady-state condition is achieved, i.e.

$$n_1 \langle c_1 \rangle = n_2 \langle c_2 \rangle,$$

with $(n_1 + n_2) = 2n$ since a fixed mass of gas is involved.

Kinetic theory shows that $(\langle c \rangle)^2 \propto \langle c^2 \rangle \propto T$, from which it is easy to establish that

$$n_1/n_2 = (T_2/T_1)^{1/2}.$$

Use of this identity in conjunction with the equations $p = bnT$ and $(n_1 + n_2) = 2n$ leads first to p_1/p_2 and then $(p_1 - p_2)$ expressed in terms of the original pressure p.

HK19   Although the gas in A is compressed slowly and adiabatically, this problem *cannot* be solved by applying $pV^\gamma = $ constant to the gas in A because the mass of gas in A does not remain constant.

The equation of state for an ideal gas can be applied to A and B separately before the change and to A and B combined after the change if careful consideration is given to the number of moles of gas involved in each case (see question HK18). The first part of the question will provide the other equation you need, i.e. a relationship between the work done on the gas and increase in thermal energy.

[It is important to realise that, since work is done on the gas, its temperature will rise. If therefore p is kept constant, the gas must occupy a bigger volume. Hence, the final total volume occupied by the gas is greater than V.

$C_{V,m}$ has not been given as a catch. Although the change occurs at constant pressure, the correct specific heat capacity to use in this problem is $C_{V,m}$. Consider carefully why this is so.]

HK20   (a) This follows directly from $p = \rho \langle c^2 \rangle / 3$.

(b) Set up two simultaneous equations, one giving the total distance travelled (i.e. the length of the line), the other giving the effective distance travelled, x. Solve these equations for n and λ.

(c) Note that molecules will collide if they are closer together than d (not r). The expression given is thus the volume swept out by one molecule between collisions and so is also a measure of the volume that 'belongs' exclusively to that molecule.

(d) The volume derived is 500 times the volume occupied in the liquid phase—approximately d^3. Note that, since this is an order-of-magnitude calculation, small numerical factors (such as $\pi/6$ here) are normally neglected.

(e) In parts (c) and (d), d is reduced (λ increased) by the size of the air molecules but it is increased (λ reduced) by molecular structure.

The speed of the air molecules has little effect on the collision probability or on λ. Simplifying assumptions in the argument will introduce errors greater than any of the above.

HK21   For part (a), the change in momentum when a force F acts for time τ is $F\tau$. Note that the question asks for the mean drift velocity, not the velocity acquired between collisions.

Part (b) is obtained by combining an expression for the force on an electron in an electric field E with two less well known equations:

(i) current density $j = nev$ (verify this) and (ii) conductivity $\sigma = j/E$ (show that this important equation may be derived from Ohm's law).

In part (c), molecular kinetic theory must be used to find the mean speed of the molecules c, whence τ may be found as λ/c.

The final part simply draws together the earlier parts into a numerical solution.

HK22   In this region of the atmosphere the density of the gas is so low that you need have no doubt about assuming ideal gas behaviour. Combine the ideal gas equation with the expression for density to obtain a relation for p in terms of ρ, R, T and M, the mass of one mole. (Remember that the statement that the relative atomic mass of oxygen $= 16$ means that the mass of one mole is 0.016 kg.) The volume occupied by each atom of oxygen is given by the volume occupied by one mole divided by the number of atoms in a mole. On average, the distance between atoms is the cube root of the volume occupied by each atom.

The kinetic theory concept of temperature is that it is measured by the average kinetic energy per atom. The same idea applies here but, where the pressure is very low, it may take a comparatively long time for thermal equilibrium to be established between the atmosphere and whatever thermometer is used to indicate the temperature.

HK23   First sketch the stages of the process (as in Fig. HK23.1) and tabulate the values of p and V. The unknown values are readily obtained using Boyle's law.

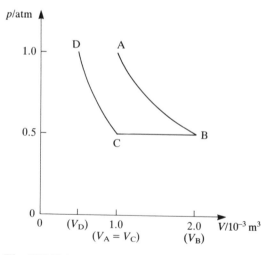

Fig. HK23.1

State	p/atm	$V/10^{-3}\,m^3$	T
A	1	1	T_1
B	0.5	2	T_1
C	0.5	1	T_2
D	1	0.5	T_2

At all stages, the state of the gas is described by $pV = nRT$, where there is an amount n, in moles, of gas.

The work done *on* the gas from A to B is

$$\int_{V_1}^{V_2} p\,dV = -nRT \ln(V_2/V_1)$$

$$= -p_A V_A \ln(V_B/V_A)$$

The work done on the gas from B to C is $p_B(V_B - V_C)$. The work done on the gas from C to D is $p_C V_C \ln(V_C/V_D)$.

Remembering that $1\,atm = 1.01 \times 10^5\,Pa$, substitution of the pressure and volume values gives the work done in each stage. Addition, with due regard to the sign, gives the total work done on the gas. Note the negative sign in the first stage: here the gas is expanding against the atmosphere and so doing work on it. Thus, the work done *on* the gas is negative.

Since the gas is ideal, internal energy is a function of temperature only. Hence, there is no change in internal energy along the isothermals AB and CD: the only change in internal energy is that associated with the transition from B to C. We expect the change to be *negative*, as the temperature T_2 at C is half the temperature T_1 at B.

The first law of thermodynamics states that the change in internal energy is given by the work done *on* the gas plus the heat supplied *to* it. Here, we have calculated the work done on the gas as 50.5 J and are told that 126 J of heat are removed during this stage; thus, the change in internal energy is $(50.5 - 126)J = -75.5\,J$.

This change in internal energy can be obtained in another way. For an ideal monatomic gas, the internal energy of an amount, n moles, at temperature T is $(3/2)nRT$. The change in internal energy between states B and C is thus $(3/2)nR(T_1 - T_2) = (3/2)(p_B V_B - p_C V_C)$. Substitute the values and check that the answer agrees with that obtained previously.

HK24 BC corresponds to a sudden increase in pressure, with no change in volume. This would occur for example when a steam valve was opened.

DA is a sudden drop in pressure creating a near-vacuum with no change in volume—perhaps the result of rapid condensation of steam due to injection of cold water.

The theoretical output of work per cycle is the area enclosed by the p–V curve. Take the lower values of p and V equal to zero and, in calculating the power, note that there is only one cycle every 5 s.

Notice also that, as the data are given, when calculating the efficiency as a percentage of the theoretical maximum the duration of the cycle is unimportant.

HK25 Deduce from $pV = k$ that $p\Delta V = -V\Delta p$. Remember that $\Delta V = A\Delta l$ and the net force is $A\Delta p$. Allowing for changes in pressure on both sides of the piston, after a small displacement, the restoring force is $2A^2 p\Delta l/V$. Hence, an equation of the type $\ddot{x} = -\omega^2 x$ can be derived to describe the motion of the piston. Remember $T = 2\pi/\omega$ and compare with $T = 2\pi(L/g)^{1/2}$, where L is the length of the equivalent simple pendulum.

HK26 The changes of internal energy in the two methods are the same because the initial and final states are the same in each. Similarly, the mechanical work done by the system is the same in each method, because the net work done on the atmosphere must be the same if the initial and final states are identical.* Apply the first law of thermodynamics to show that the inputs of thermal energy must be the same in each method.

Calculate the specific latent heat of vaporisation by writing the equations for the input of thermal energy in each method. From the argument above, these inputs are equal.

The specific latent heat of vaporisation at 20 °C is appreciably greater than that at 100 °C because, on average, liquid molecules are closer together at the lower temperature, so that the intermolecular forces are stronger.

(*Assuming the changes take place slowly and reversibly.)

Electrostatics

ES1 This is a piece of physics that used to be a standard part of any electromagnetism course because magnetism was taught from the starting point of a short bar magnet with a N-pole at one end and S-pole at the other (the analogy should be obvious). This approach is taught much less frequently now but is nevertheless important because, among other things, it helps to describe the behaviour of molecules with permanent dipole moments. Since all dielectric materials polarise slightly in an electric field to give induced dipoles, the approach is also useful for describing many of the properties of induced dipoles.

In case (c), the electric field E at distance r from O due to Q is

$$\frac{Q}{4\pi\varepsilon_0(r-a)^2},$$

and the potential due to that charge can be obtained from

$$E = -\frac{\mathrm{d}\phi}{\mathrm{d}r}.$$

If the distance from P to Q is written $r(1 - a/r)$, the binomial expansion may be used where necessary, and this will simplify the algebra when adding the effect of $-Q$. Note that, because electric fields are vectors whereas potentials are scalars, each of these quantities must be added accordingly (the point of the first part of the question).

The most general way to answer the next part is to place the dipole at some angle θ to the field and write down the work done to turn it through a small angle $\mathrm{d}\theta$. Integrating from $\theta = 0$ rad to π rad will give the required answer.

ES2 This question is a good example of the application of Gauss' theorem. Try to think of the theorem as 'the total normal induction over any closed surface is equal to the total charge enclosed by that surface'.

Mathematically,

$$\int \mathbf{D} \cdot d\mathbf{S} = \sum Q.$$

(This is a vector dot product, which means that only the component of $\mathbf{D}$ normal to the surface, i.e. parallel to the vector $d\mathbf{S}$, which is used to represent a small surface area, is relevant.)

Since $\mathbf{D} = \varepsilon_r \varepsilon_0 \mathbf{E}$, in free space, where $\varepsilon_r = 1$,

$$\int \varepsilon_0 \mathbf{E} \cdot d\mathbf{S} = \sum Q.$$

For a spherical enclosing surface of radius r, (i) E is the same for all values of r, so it can be taken outside the integration sign and denoted by E_r, (ii) $d\mathbf{S}$ is just the total surface area, i.e. $4\pi r^2$.

Hence

$$4\pi r^2 \varepsilon_0 E_r = \sum Q.$$

Clearly, when r is less than a, $\sum Q$ varies with r if the charge is spread throughout the sphere but, for $r \geqslant a$, $\sum Q$ is constant. [Apply this idea to the qualitative part of the question at the end also.]

By using $E = -d\phi/dr$ and doing a simple integration, you should be able to show that (provided $r \geqslant a$) ϕ varies as $1/r$. Remember to take zero potential at infinity. Care is required to calculate the potential when $r < a$. Write

$$\phi_r = \int_a^r -E_r\, dr + C,$$

take care with the signs, and use the value of ϕ at $r = a$ from the previous part of your answer to find C (since ϕ must have the same value at $r = a$ whichever expression is used).

ES3 First, show that the horizontal field gives each type of powder particle a horizontal acceleration of $0.4\,\mathrm{m\,s^{-2}}$. Then find the time to travel $0.05\,\mathrm{m}$ (not $0.1\,\mathrm{m}$!). During this time, the particles are falling freely under gravity.

Numerous assumptions are made—no air resistance, no attraction between falling separated charged particles, no initial speed, no edge effects.

ES4   For part (a), recall that the electric field at R will be given by the force on unit positive charge placed at R. However, the effect of q and its 'image' must be added vectorially.

For part (c), note that the planes are replaced by three image charges, not two, and that the total force must again be obtained by vector addition.

For part (d), one approach is to write down the force on q at a general distance x from the plates (note that q and all its images will approach the plates at the same rate), equate this force to mass × acceleration, and integrate.

The same answer can be obtained by considering conservation of energy.

ES5   If you do not know that the electric field E a distance x from the axis of a wire bearing a uniform distribution of charge σ per unit length is $E = \sigma/2\pi\varepsilon_0 x$, this can easily be derived using Gauss' law. The direction of the field is radially outwards. The field in an insulator of relative permittivity ε_r is $E_1 = \sigma/2\pi\varepsilon_0\varepsilon_r x$. The graph of E against x thus consists of two segments of a $1/x$ curve.

The field E and potential V are related by $E = -\,\mathrm{d}V/\mathrm{d}x$, so the potential can be obtained by integrating the expression for the field between $x = r$ and $x = R$. You will need to know that the integral of k/x between $x = a$ and $x = b$ is $k\ln(b/a)$.

ES6   Use Coulomb's law to calculate the electric field at P due to the point charge δQ at S. To find the total field due to the total charge on the loop, add up the contributions from elements similar to S all round the loop. The components of these contributions normal to the axis will cancel out; the sum of the components along the axis is equal to the total field. The field an infinite distance from the loop is zero; it is also zero at O, in the plane of the loop. It must therefore have a maximum value somewhere in between. If you want to verify the statement in the question about the position of the point where the field is a maximum, differentiate your expression for E and put $\mathrm{d}E/\mathrm{d}x = 0$.

To find the potential at P, start by writing down the potential due to the point charge δQ. Remember that potential is a scalar: to find the total potential, add up the contributions from elements all round the loop without taking components. The potential is a maximum at the point O, the closest possible point to all elements of charge on the loop.

From the potential expression V, you can easily obtain the potential energy of an electron at the point P by multiplying V by $-e$. Find the potential energies at the point of release and at the centre of the loop. From the principle of conservation of energy, this

reduction in potential energy is equal to the increase in kinetic energy
of the electron. Equate the changes in energy and rearrange to find
the expression for v^2. The electron will move through the loop and
will oscillate backwards and forwards. Note that the oscillations are
not simple harmonic, because the restoring force due to the electric
field is not proportional to the displacement.

ES7 (a) Apply ideas of symmetry. To calculate V, note that all the charge
is at a distance $(r^2 + x^2)^{1/2}$ from P and also recall that potential is
a scalar. By symmetry, E must act along the x axis and may be
obtained by differentiating V with respect to x (take care with signs).

(b) If the charge is uniformly distributed, the charge density is
$q/\pi r^2$ and the disc can be considered as a set of annuli, each of radius
y and thickness dy.

The potential at P due to each annulus may be obtained as in
part (a) and the total potential found by integration.

The substitutions $y^2 + x^2 = z$ and $2y\,dy = dz$ will be useful and
should lead to an integral of the form $\int k\,dz/z^{1/2}$.

(c) E may be obtained by differentiation as in the first part. When
$x \gg r$, expansion of the expression for E by the binomial theorem
leads to $E = q/4\pi\varepsilon_0 x^2$: this expression for E is the same as that
predicted by Gauss' theorem for the potential at a point a distance
x from a point charge.

When $x \ll r, E = q/2\pi\varepsilon_0 r^2$, this being the value of E close to an
isolated infinite sheet of insulator.

ES8 If the torsion constant of the wire is μ, then the torsional couple
in the first part is $0.25\,\mu$. This is equal to the torsional couple due
to the repulsive force between the charges, $q^2 l/4\pi\varepsilon_0 r^2$ (don't overlook
the l in the numerator).

A similar equation applies to the second part and the unknowns
can be eliminated to give a cubic equation in θ, i.e.

$$\theta^2(0.5 - \theta) = (0.25)^3.$$

This could be solved, but it suffices to show by substitution that
$\theta = 0.4$ rad is a solution.

To show that the second position is one of stable equilibrium,
write down separate values for the torsion couple G_1 and the couple
due to the electrostatic force G_2. Then, by considering the change
$dG/d\theta$ for each of these couples when the wire is twisted by a small
amount, show that they will act to restore equilibrium, i.e. it is stable.

There are two other roots to the equation, which should
correspond to physical states of equilibrium if θ is real.

ES9 The intensity of the electric field may be found in each region by Gauss' theorem. Starting from the upper plate, imagine Gaussian surfaces that (i) end above the sheets of ions, (ii) enclose the upper sheet of ions, (iii) enclose both sheets of ions.

Your sketch should then be as shown in Fig. ES9.2.

The corresponding sketch for V (Fig. ES9.3) may be obtained from $E = -dV/dx$. Thus, the change in V with distance is the same in regions (i) and (iii). V changes more slowly between the sheets of ions but still decreases because E is still positive.

The potential difference between the plates is

$$-[E_1(d-x)/2 + E_2 x + E_3(d-x)/2]$$

and $C = q/V$.

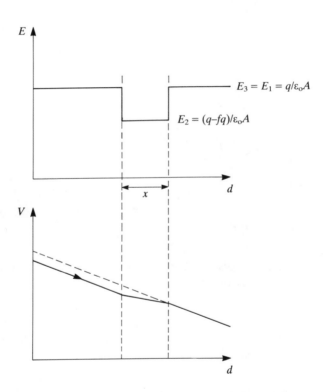

ES9.2

$E_3 = E_1 = q/\varepsilon_o A$

$E_2 = (q-fq)/\varepsilon_o A$

ES9.3

ES10 There are a number of basic equations that you must know if you wish to solve questions of this type simply and quickly. They are summarised below.

(1) The electric field intensity, $E = -V/x$, if constant, or $E = -(dV/dx)$, if varying.

(2) The electric displacement D and electric field intensity E are related by $D = \varepsilon_r \varepsilon_0 E$.

(3) The normal component of the electric displacement has the same value on each side of an uncharged boundary.

(4) This is really a special case of Gauss' theorem, which states that the total normal induction over any surface is equal to the charge within.

In the situation shown in Fig. ES10.1,

$$D_{\text{out}}A - D_{\text{in}}A = \sigma A$$

(be careful with the signs). Hence $D_{\text{out}} - D_{\text{in}} = \sigma$, which becomes (a) $D_{\text{out}} = D_{\text{in}}$, if σ is zero, (b) $E_{\text{out}} - E_{\text{in}} = \sigma/\varepsilon_0$, if there is air on both sides of the charged surface, since ε_r (air) ≈ 1.

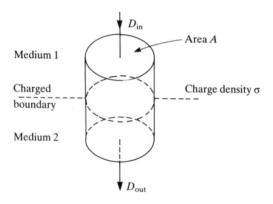

Fig. ES10.1

These equations give all the necessary information to solve this problem and many other problems of this type.

ES11   Remember that the capacitance of a parallel-plate capacitor of area A and plate separation d is $\varepsilon_r \varepsilon_0 A/d$. If in difficulty, refer to the general advice in question ES10.

ES12   The problem is best approached by conservation of energy. If the plates are of length l and separation d, and the liquid rises to an equilibrium height of h, the volume of liquid between the plates is ldh, its mass is $ldh\rho$ and its potential energy is $(ldh\rho g)h/2$ (the centre of gravity only rises $h/2$!).

This energy must come from the electrical energy of the system. Since the capacitor is charged to 1000 V *and then isolated*, the charge

Q on its plates remains constant. Small changes in energy can be written

$$\Delta(Q^2/2C) = -(Q^2/2C^2)\Delta C$$

if h is assumed to be small. Note that when ΔC is positive $-(Q^2/2C^2)\Delta C$ is negative, so the system *loses* electrical energy as required if it gains potential energy.

Now

$$\Delta C = (\varepsilon_r - 1)\varepsilon_0 hl/d,$$

since air space in the capacitor is being replaced by liquid, and $Q/C = V$.

So

$$ldh\rho gh/2 = V^2(\varepsilon_r - 1)\varepsilon_0 hl/2d,$$

giving

$$h = \left(\frac{V}{d}\right)^2 \frac{\varepsilon_0(\varepsilon_r - 1)}{\rho g}.$$

Note that the right numerical answer can also be obtained by using the result of question ES11, in which the field energy per unit volume is shown to equal $\varepsilon_r \varepsilon_0 E^2/2$. When the liquid rises, the field energy changes from $\varepsilon_0 E^2/2$ to $\varepsilon_r \varepsilon_0 E^2/2$ in a volume ldh. This approach seems to lead to the right answer (try it and see) but gives an *increase* in field energy, which cannot also provide the required mechanical energy. The fallacy in this approach is that, if the capacitor is isolated, and the total charge is constant, there is a redistribution of charge when the liquid enters the capacitor, and thus the field energy changes in the air space as well as in the liquid. Alternatively, if the capacitor is left connected to the battery so that the field in the air space remains constant, the charge on the plates increases and the battery has to supply extra electrical energy. From the preceding discussion you should be able to work out very quickly exactly how much energy the battery would supply.

ES13 A drawing will help for the first part (Fig. ES13.1). Show from first principles that, for the capacitor filled with dielectric considered alone, its capacitance is $\varepsilon_0 \varepsilon_r ax/d$. Then explain carefully why the system behaves like two capacitors in parallel.

For the second part, the rate of loss of charge can be related both to the rate of change of capacitance and to the resistance in the circuit. The rest is substitution.

Finally, show that the resistance of the dielectric is $d/\sigma ax$. Then,

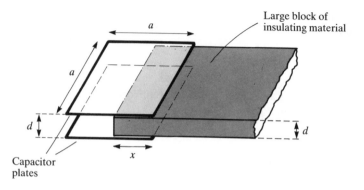

Fig. ES13.1

by combining the two resistances in parallel, you can show that the condition for V to be constant is the differential equation

$$[\varepsilon_0 a(\varepsilon_r - 1)/d]\,\mathrm{d}x/\mathrm{d}t = \sigma ax/d + 1/R.$$

Since $\mathrm{d}x/\mathrm{d}t$ now varies with x, there is no constant value.

ES14 Each of these sections follows logically from the previous one. The general advice in question ES10 and some of the equations in the advice to question ES12 may help.

ES15 A very effective method to calculate the capacitance of a regular surface is illustrated here for the sphere.

(a) Put a charge $+q$ on the surface of the sphere.

(b) Write down Gauss' theorem for an arbitrary radius r outside the sphere, i.e.

$$\varepsilon_0 E 4\pi r^2 = q.$$

(c) Set $E = -\mathrm{d}V/\mathrm{d}r$.

(d) Rearranging then gives

$$(4\pi\varepsilon_0/q)\,\mathrm{d}V = -\mathrm{d}r/r^2.$$

(e) Integration from $r = a$ to $r = \infty$ gives $4\pi\varepsilon_0 V/q = 1/a$.

(f) $C = q/V = 4\pi\varepsilon_0 a$.

For the last part, first explain why there is no field energy inside the sphere.

Divide up the space outside the sphere into spherical shells, a typical shell at radius r having thickness $\mathrm{d}r$.

$E = Q/4\pi r^2 \varepsilon_0$ as above, and the volume of this shell is $4\pi r^2\,\mathrm{d}r$.

Hence, the field energy of this shell is

$$(\varepsilon_0/2)(Q/4\pi r^2 \varepsilon_0)^2 4\pi r^2\,\mathrm{d}r.$$

The total field energy becomes an integral of the form $\int kx^{-2}\,dx$ and leads to a value of $Q^2/8\pi\varepsilon_0 a$, which is consistent with $Q^2/2C$.

ES16 There are several ways to answer the first part. One possibility is to consider the electric field.

Without the dielectric, if the area of the capacitor plates is $A, E = Q/\varepsilon_0 A, V = Qd/\varepsilon_0 A$ (d = plate separation) and

$$C = Q/V = \varepsilon_0 A/d.$$

The presence of the dielectric is equivalent to a charge $-Q'$ on the upper plate. Hence,

$$E' = (Q - Q')/\varepsilon_0 A,$$

$$V' = (Q - Q')d/\varepsilon_0 A,$$

$$C' = \frac{Q}{V'} = \frac{Q}{(Q - Q')}\frac{\varepsilon_0 A}{d}$$

and

$$\varepsilon_r = C'/C = Q/(Q - Q').$$

For the final part, show from simple theory that a graph of $(Q/C)^{-1}$ against d/m should be a straight line. Note that, for large values of d, the simple theory may not hold because of edge effects.

ES17 The important step in the first part is to show that the energy dissipated in the resistor is $CV^2/2$. One way is to consider an intermediate situation where the capacitor is at potential v and carries charge q. Find the work required to drive a small charge δq through the resistor and then integrate to find the work done in driving a finite charge Q through the resistor.

In the second part, consider, separately, the energy taken from the battery, stored in the capacitor, and dissipated in the resistor. Any 'spare energy' is work done in the oil. Note that, when the oil flows in slowly, there will also be a slow continuous flow of charge. When the oil flows in quickly (assume no charge flows during this time), a finite potential difference will be established across the resistor and some energy will be dissipated as heat. You should be able to show that the work done on the oil by the electrical system is CV^2 in part (i) but only $CV^2/3$ in part (ii).

Note that there are many ways of stating the second law of thermodynamics, and this problem illustrates one of them, namely that the maximum amount of useful work that can be obtained from any change is when it is carried out slowly (reversibly). If the same change is done quickly (irreversibly), a greater amount of energy is wasted as heat.

Current electricity

E1 The resistance R_c of a piece of constantan wire of length L_c at a temperature θ is given by

$$R_c = L_c r_c (1 + \alpha_c \theta),$$

where r_c is the resistance per unit length at $0\,^\circ\text{C}$. There is a similar expression for the resistance R_m of a piece of manganin wire. The total resistance of the two wires in series is $R_c + R_m$. Write down this expression and note that it has a term in θ. If the total resistance is to be independent of temperature, the coefficient of θ in the expression must be zero. Apply this condition, and obtain the ratio L_c/L_m of the lengths of constantan and manganin wire in any resistor that has a resistance independent of temperature. Then find the lengths required for a resistor of resistance $5.0\,\Omega$.

E2 (a) The first part of this question provides an opportunity to introduce a useful variation of Ohm's law. For any conductor of length l and cross-sectional area A carrying current, we may write $V = IR$ in usual notation. Now (i) the current density $j = I/A$, (ii) the electric field E in the wire (assumed uniform) is related to V by $E = -V/l$, (iii) $R = \rho l/A$, where ρ is the resistivity. By using the expressions in (i), (ii) and (iii) to substitute for I, V and R, it follows that $E = -j\rho$. If you apply these ideas you should be able to answer the first part of the question very neatly.

(b) In the second part, start from an equation $P = V^2/R$ for the power dissipation and note that the total resistance is $(\rho_1 + \rho_2)h/A$. This part should then be fairly straightforward.

E3 Write down the Kirchhoff equations for the cases when X is connected to A, B and C in turn.

When X is at A:

$$I = I_1 + I_2,$$

$$I_2(R_1 + R_2 + R_3) - I_1 r = 0.$$

When X is at B:

$$I' = I_1 + I'_2,$$

$$I'_2(R_2 + R_3) - I_1(R_1 + r) = 0.$$

When X is at C:

$$I'' = I_1 + I''_2,$$

$$I''_2 R_3 - I_1(R_1 + R_2 + r) = 0.$$

Substitute $I_1 = 2 \times 10^{-4}\,\text{A}$, $I_2 = 1 \times 10^{-3}\,\text{A}$, $I'_2 = 1 \times 10^{-2}\,\text{A}$, $I''_2 = 1 \times 10^{-1}\,\text{A}$ and $r = 500\,\Omega$, and solve.

E4 Show that, when the voltmeter is connected across R, the total resistance of the circuit is

$$R_x + \frac{Rr}{R + r}.$$

Hence find relationships between (i) the e.m.f. E of the battery and the current in the circuit, (ii) the voltmeter reading V_R and the current in the circuit. Eliminate the current from these relationships to show that

$$\frac{E}{V_R} = \frac{R_x R + R_x r + Rr}{Rr}$$

(it is helpful to notice the symmetry of this expression).

With a similar pair of equations written down when the voltmeter is across R_x (noting that the current is now different), the solution follows.

In the last part, note the words *in italics*. It is true that voltmeters are usually connected across resistors, not in series with them, but this problem shows one possible way to find the internal resistance of a voltmeter. The remainder of the calculation follows the same ideas as the first part.

E5 There are many ways to solve this problem. The following is perhaps the most direct.

(a) Use Kirchhoff's law to show that each short length of double wire of resistance $r/2$ takes current $2I$, so the heating effect is the same as for two separate wires, each carrying current I.

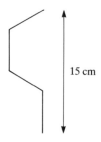

15 cm

Fig. E5.2

Hence the whole of the hexagonal array is made up of single strands of wire with the repeat unit shown in Fig. E5.2. The effective length of the repeat unit is 15 cm, the length of wire being 20 cm.

(b) Find the total length of wire in one strand between the conducting bars.

(c) Use the fact that there are two strands at intervals of $5\sqrt{3}$ cm to find the total number of strands, n.

(d) Use the values given for power dissipated and voltage to find the resistance R of the network and hence the resistance for a single strand R_s, of which there are n in parallel (not in series!)

(e) Substitute calculated or given values in $R_s = \rho l/A$ to find the cross-sectional area of each wire and hence its diameter.

E6 Note that the sum of the p.d.'s across the two components must be 6 V at all times. Show that in part (b) the ratio of the p.d. s across the two components must be 2.

E7 The resistance of an annulus of the screen at radius r with thicknesses δr and t must be obtained in terms of the resistivity. Remember, when using $R = \rho l/A$, that l is measured *along the direction of current flow*. If further help is required, refer to the advice for question E8. An integration of the form $\int k \, dx/x$ is involved.

This p.d. is negligible compared with the p.d. required to deflect the spot.

E8 Although the resistance, or capacitance, of a body is an inherent property of that body, it is usually necessary to establish a potential difference before the resistance (or capacitance) can be calculated. For example, a good start to this problem is to think of a potential difference existing between the hemisphere and the tank, and then to decide which way the current will flow and why. Apply the standard equation $R = \rho l/A$ to the region between the hemispherical shells, remembering that l is the dimension *along the direction of* *current flow* (see advice to question E7). An integral of the form $\int k \, dx/x^2$ is involved.

The position of maximum rate of temperature rise is obviously close to the metal hemisphere if you think carefully about how the electrical energy on the hemisphere must be dissipated. Find the rate of power dissipation in a thin shell at this radius and equate this rate to $mc \, d\theta/dt$.

One final comment; see if you can reduce the final expression for $d\theta/dt$ to just *four* algebraic symbols (two are squared) before you substitute numbers. The question is an object lesson in the advantage of using symbols for as long as possible before substituting numbers.

E9 (a) (i) Show that, because the resistance of a single aluminium strand is only 1/17 that of a steel strand, an aluminium strand carries 17 times the current. This means that the current carried by any steel strand may be neglected. Now work out the resistance of 30 aluminium strands in parallel.

(ii) For fixed power transmission, $IV = $ constant, i.e. V is proportional to $1/I$. But power losses depend on I^2; they accordingly vary as $1/V^2$ and are thus reduced by large V.

(iii) If 55 MW are transmitted at 132 kV, the current in the power-line is 380 A. Then use the relationship:

$$\text{power loss/power transmitted} = I^2 R/VI.$$

(iv) Try to show that, because of differences in the Young modulus and in the number of strands, the tensile stress at fixed extension will be about 10 to 12 times greater in the steel core. The steel core can withstand the greater stress because its breaking stress is so much greater.

(b) (i) By considering a simple phasor diagram (Fig. E9.1), the difference in r.m.s. voltage, ΔV, is given by $(V_1 - V_2)$ and this is $\sqrt{3}V$.

(ii) If the loads on each phase wire are equal, the currents are equal. They add to give zero return current (Fig. E9.2).

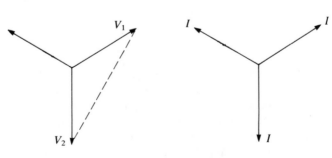

Fig. E9.1   Fig. E9.2

E10   The current I in the cables is given by $I = P/V$; hence, the power dissipated as heat is $I^2 R = P^2 R/V^2$. The power P_L delivered to the load is the input power minus the power dissipated as heat. Beware of the error of taking the power lost as heat to be V^2/R: this assumes that the potential drop across the cables alone is V (instead of across the cables and the load).

The efficiency (given by $1 - PR/V^2$) can be increased in two ways: by *decreasing* R or by *increasing* V. Decreasing the resistance could be achieved by increasing the cross-sectional area of the cables, but this would increase the mass of the cables and might lead to suspension problems. Increasing a network of pylons and cables would be expensive! The use of superconducting cables might be considered, but this would require the replacement of the existing overhead network by an underground one. Increasing the input voltage would require the replacement of generators and transformers (more expense) and, as a secondary feature, might lead to arc-over across insulators on the pylons (again, more expense).

E11   The first part of the question illustrates the very important principle that a measuring device must cause minimal disturbance to the system on which measurements are being made. For example, a device that carried a large charge could not be used to measure an electric field because the charge on the measuring instrument would create its own field. How would you avoid this problem here?

For the numerical part, plot $\ln(V/V)$ against (t/s) but explain carefully why this is the most suitable graph to plot.

E12   (a) Application of Kirchhoff's law gives $IR = v_i - v_c$, where I is the current at time t. I is also equal to dQ/dt, where the charge Q on the capacitor is given by Cv_c. Thus $v_i - v_c = RC(dv_c/dt)$, as required.

In the next part, you must either solve the differential equation you have just derived or show that the expression given in the question satisfies this differential equation. It is generally easier to adopt the second approach. Differentiating the given expression leads to

$$(dv_c/dt) = -(A/RC)\exp(-t/RC).$$

By substitution, show that this satisfies the differential equation.

If the switch is closed with the capacitor uncharged at $t = 0$, $0 = v_i + A$; hence $v_c = v_i[1 - \exp(-t/RC)]$, as required.

(b) The quantity RC is the *time constant* of the circuit, and the details of the time variation of v_c will depend on how the period T of the square-wave input v_i compares with RC. If $T \gg RC$, v_c is an almost square wave, with slight rounding of the corners, and amplitude equal to V_0. If $T = RC$, then v_c shows well-developed exponential segments; the amplitude is approximately equal to V_0. If $T \ll RC$, the exponential growth and decay does not have time to develop, and v_c shows segments of small curvature, giving an approximation to a saw-tooth wave of amplitude much less than V_0.

By symmetry, v_c starts at $+V$, falls to $-V$, and rises to $+V$ again over a cycle of period T. Fixing the zero of time arbitrarily, put $v_c = +V$ at $t = 0$; v_c will then be $-V$ at $t = T/2$. Using the expression in part (a) of the question, $v_i = -V_0$ and the constant A is $V_0 + V$. So, at $t = T/2$, we have

$$-V = -V_0 + (V_0 + V)\exp(-T/2RC),$$

which leads to the required expression.

In the last part, we are dealing with the situation $T \ll RC$. Show that, as T tends to zero, (V/V_0) tends to $T/4RC$. By substitution of the values $(V/V_0) = 0.01$ and $T = 1 \times 10^{-3}\,\text{s}$ (corresponding to a frequency of 1 kHz), show that the minimum value of RC is 0.025 s.

E13   For the first part, treat R_A and R_B as a simple potential divider.

There are several ways to do the last part. One possibility is to show (a) that the potential difference across R_A initially is $4V_0/5$, (b) that the potential difference across R_A when the diode stops conducting is $2V_0/5$. Then recall that

$$V_t = V_0 \exp(-t/RC).$$

The graphs need to be thought out very carefully. It may be useful to note (1) that while the diode is conducting, the current through R_B must stay constant because the potential difference across R_B is constant, (2) when the diode stops conducting, the current through R_A will show a discontinuity because the time constant of the circuit suddenly changes.

For further guidance, see question E12.

E14   Your sketches should look like those in Fig. E14.4.

Note the following points.

(i) The sum of V_R and V_C must be 5 V at all times up to 0.02 s and must be zero at all subsequent times.

(ii) The time constant is 0.01 s (CR); accordingly, after 0.02 s, V_R decreases to 0.68 V.

For further guidance on the first part, see question E12.

In the second part, recognise that at any instant the current I through the resistor is equal to the rate of change of charge on the capacitor. Hence, if $Q = CV_C$ instantaneously, then $I = dQ/dt = C\,dV_C/dt$.

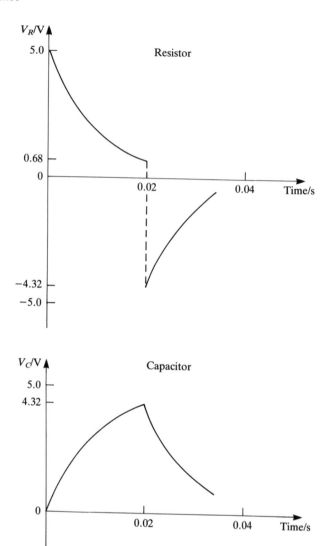

Fig. E14.4

The required answer for the differentiating circuit,

$$V_{out} = - RC\,dV_{in}/dt,$$

follows directly from application of the above ideas.

When the resistor and capacitor are interchanged, it becomes an integrating circuit. $Q = - CV_{out}$ and $I = V_{in}/R$. Since $I = dQ/dt$, $Q = \int I\,dt$, etc. The output voltage is now proportional to the time integral of the input voltage.

Examples of uses of these circuits are

(i) analysis of differential equations in analogue computers,

(ii) use of an integrating circuit with search coil and oscilloscope for *B*-field measurement.

E15 To answer part (a) correctly, you must read the question carefully and be clear which phase angle is required. Remember that the p.d. across a resistor is always in phase with the current through it.

Most of the ideas needed to answer the last part should be familiar to you. A few reminders are listed below in case you are in difficulty.

(1) What is the instantaneous flux through the coil?

(2) What is the induced e.m.f. (rate of cutting lines of flux) due to rotation of the coil?

(3) What is the impedance of a resistor and capacitor in series?

(4) What is the time average value of a function that is varying sinusoidally? What is the time average of the square of the function?

E16 The current in the $R - C$ series circuit falls exponentially with time after the switch is closed. The time constant of the decay is RC. Thus, the potential difference across the resistor also falls exponentially. By Kirchhoff's law, the potential difference across the capacitor rises according to the relation

$$V_C = V[1 - \exp(-t/RC)].$$

Use this equation to find an expression, in terms of R and C, for the time for the potential difference across the capacitor (and the neon lamp) to rise from zero to 45 V. Hence find the value of R for the neon lamp to flash at the required rate.

The power drawn from the battery is all dissipated in the resistor. At time t, the current is $(V/R)\exp(-t/RC)$ and, between t and $t + \mathrm{d}t$, the energy dissipated as heat is $[(V^2/R)\exp(-2t/RC)]\,\mathrm{d}t$. To obtain the mean power, integrate this expression over a complete flashing cycle and divide by the period of the cycle.

For further relevant advice, see the guidance for question E17.

E17 Since current is a rate of flow of charge, the current through the neon tube can be related to the rate of loss of charge from the capacitor. Also since $q = CV$,

$$\frac{\mathrm{d}q}{\mathrm{d}t} = C\frac{\mathrm{d}V}{\mathrm{d}t}.$$

Equating the two values for dq/dt, substituting the numerical value for C, rearranging and changing the limits of the integration to allow for the minus sign gives

$$t = \frac{1}{2.62} \int_{157}^{220} \frac{dV}{(V - 147)}.$$

For the last part, the charging process can be described by

$$V = V_0[1 - \exp(-t/RC)].$$

Your final sketch should resemble Fig. E17.2.

For further advice, see question E16 and the guidance for that question.

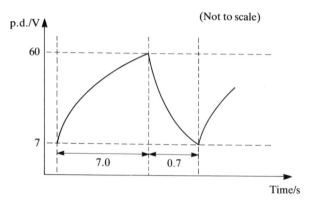

Fig. E17.2

E18 (a) Recall that conductivity is the reciprocal of resistivity and refer to the guidance for question E2.

(b) One expression for the drift velocity can be written in terms of: j, the current density; n, the number of free electrons per unit volume; and the magnitude e of the electron charge. Another relates the drift velocity to: E, the applied electric field; t, the mean time between collisions; and m_e, the mass of the electron. They combine to give

$$t = 2m_e \sigma / ne^2.$$

(c) The electron thermal speed may be estimated by equating the electron kinetic energy to $3kT/2$. λ follows directly if this result is combined with the time between collisions.

On the basis of this calculation, the electrons travel about 10 atomic diameters between impacts. However, both the random motion of the electrons and also λ are dependent on T: as T increases, both of these will change in such a way as to reduce the drift velocity of the electrons and hence reduce the conductivity.

E19 The first part of the question is a straightforward application of the equation $I = nAve$, where I is the current in a wire of cross-sectional area A, n is the number density of free electrons (the number per unit volume) and v is their drift velocity.

If the wire is carrying an alternating current, the instantaneous value of the current, and hence of the drift velocity, will vary periodically. The maximum value of the drift velocity is

$$v_{max} = I_{max}/nAe.$$

The electrons in the wire oscillate with simple harmonic motion. From the properties of s.h.m., $v_{max} = a\omega$, where a is the amplitude of the motion and ω is the angular frequency. Thus, the amplitude of oscillation of the free electrons is given by $I_{max}/nAe\omega$.

The application of the electrical signal sets the free electrons into oscillation, and the pulse is transmitted along the wire by these coupled oscillations. The oscillations are equivalent to the periodic variation of electric and magnetic fields, that is, to an electromagnetic wave travelling with a speed approaching c.

Electromagnetism

EM1 The force per unit length between parallel current-carrying conductors is given by

$$F/l = \mu_0 I_1 I_2 / 2\pi d,$$

where I_1 and I_2 are the currents in the conductors, which are separated by a distance d. Here the peak currents $I_1 = I_2 = 3.0\,(2)^{1/2} \sin 100\,\pi t$. Note the $(2)^{1/2}$ factor to convert the r.m.s. current to a peak value and the conversion of 50 Hz to $100\,\pi$ rad s^{-1}. Also note carefully the shape of the $\sin^2(100\pi t)$ curve.

EM2 Refer to Fig. EM2.1. The flux density of the magnetic field due to the straight wire at a distance r from the wire is given by $B = \mu_0 I_1 / 2\pi r$.

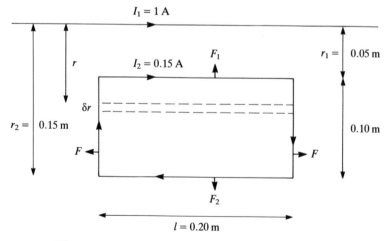

Fig. EM2.1

The force acting on the side of the loop nearer to the straight wire is given by $F_1 = B_1 I_2 l = \mu_0 I_1 I_2 l / 2\pi r_1$. This force acts at right angles to both B_1 and I_2, that is, in the horizontal plane and towards the straight wire. The force on the further parallel wire is one of repulsion and is given by $\mu_0 I_1 I_2 l / 2\pi r_2$.

The force on the shorter sides would be more difficult to calculate, as r is no longer constant along the length of these sides. It could be obtained by integration; but the force on each of the shorter sides is equal in magnitude but opposite in direction (outwards), so the net effect due to these forces is zero.

Substitute the values in the question to obtain a net force of 8.0×10^{-8} N, directed towards the straight wire.

In order to find the induced e.m.f. as the current in the straight wire is reduced to zero, we have to find the rate of change of flux linked with the rectangular loop. Divide the loop into strips parallel to the longer sides. The flux through the strip shown is $\mu_0 I_1 L \delta r / 2\pi r$. Integration between the limits of $r = 0.05$ m and $r = 0.15$ m gives the total flux Φ as $(\mu_0 I_1 \times 0.2 \ln 3)/2\pi$. The induced e.m.f. is equal to the rate of change of flux linkage dΦ/dt. Substituting the values in the question gives an e.m.f. of 4.4×10^{-6} V. From Lenz's law, this e.m.f. will act so as to oppose the cause of the change producing the e.m.f. That is, it will try to maintain the original force between the wire and the loop by generating a current in the loop so that it flows in the same direction in the nearer wire of the loop as the current in the straight wire.

EM3 Considering the current in the lower rod, the magnetic flux density at P is $\mu_0 I / 2\pi y$. There is a similar term for the magnetic flux density due to the current in the upper rod, $\mu_0 I / 2\pi (D - y)$. Because the currents are in opposite directions, the resultant flux density at P is given by the sum of these two terms.

To find the magnetic flux through the area WXYZ, divide this area into elements of width dy parallel to ZY. Use the relation $\Phi = BA$ to find the flux dΦ through the element of area Ldy at a distance y from ZY, containing the point P. Integrate this expression from $y = r$ to $y = (D - r)$ to find the total flux through WXYZ.

The self-inductance L is obtained from the relation $\Phi = IL$.

EM4 The principle that is used to calculate the magnetic flux density outside the wire can also be applied inside the wire. The lines of magnetic field intensity inside the wire are closed circles concentric with the axis of the wire but only that part of the current enclosed by the loop of radius a can contribute to B. Good analogies are the electric field intensity due to distributed charge and the gravitational field intensity due to distributed mass.

For the last part, show that in the high-frequency case the current density $j (= I/A)$ and the effective resistance $R (= \rho l/A)$ are both $a/2x$ times the corresponding values when the current is uniformly distributed.

The heating effect can then be calculated either by using the standard I^2R formula, or by writing down the heating effect in terms of j, ρ and the total volume through which current flows.

EM5 The record can be considered as divided into a series of rings. Consider one ring, radius r and thickness δr. The rotation of the charge δQ within this ring is equivalent to a current. Show that the magnetic flux density at the centre of the record, δB, due to this ring is given by

$$\delta B = \frac{\mu_0 \delta Q \omega}{2r}.$$

Substitute the value of Q and the total magnetic flux density follows by integration of a very simple expression of the form $\int k \, dx$.

Consider what will happen to the charge if the disc is a good conductor and then go on to show that this charge redistribution makes a factor of two difference to the magnetic flux density at the centre of the gramophone record.

EM6 For a coil with square sides of length a and n turns, the torque $= na^2BI$.

However, if the total length of wire l is fixed, $a = l/4n$, and the rest follows.

EM7 At an arbitrary instant, let the plane of the coil make an angle θ with the magnetic field. The flux through the coil at that instant is accordingly $a^2NB \sin \theta$.

However, if the coil is rotating at angular frequency ω then, assuming $\theta = 0$ when $t = 0$, we may replace θ by ωt and the flux becomes $a^2NB \sin \omega t$.

But $E = d\Phi/dt$; hence, the e.m.f. generated is $\omega a^2NB \cos \omega t$, i.e. sinusoidal with amplitude ωa^2NB.

If the total length of wire is L and cross-sectional area α, $\alpha L = V$ and the total number of turns $N = L/4a$.

Also, the resistance of the wire $= \rho L/\alpha$ or $16a^2N^2\rho/V$ from the above relationships. The resistance of the ammeter must be added to give the total resistance in the circuit, R.

The measured current $I_{min} = $ (e.m.f. generated)$/R$.

Your sketch of B against N should show both contributions to B separately, and when they are added, a clear minimum. The minimum value of N is found by deriving an expression for dB/dN and setting it equal to zero.

EM8 The explanations required in the first part provide the method for answering the problem. If the resistor is wound inductively, its impedance $Z = (R^2 + \omega^2 L^2)^{1/2}$; if it is wound non-inductively, $Z = R$.

The heating effect, i.e. power P in the meter, is $I^2 R$ but $I = V/Z$. Thus, $V = P^{1/2} Z/R^{1/2}$ and $V \propto P^{1/2}$ provided $Z/R^{1/2}$ is a constant.

However, since $Z = (R^2 + \omega^2 L^2)^{1/2}$, this will not be true unless the calibration frequency of 1 MHz is used.

It is now most elegant to proceed by a differential method:

$$Z = (R^2 + \omega^2 L^2)^{1/2},$$
$$dZ/d\omega = (R^2 + \omega^2 L^2)^{-1/2} \omega L,$$
$$dZ/Z = 1/20 \ (5\%), \text{ etc.}$$

However, the answer will come out if Z is calculated at 1 MHz, the new value of Z for a 5% change is worked out and the corresponding value of ω calculated. Don't forget that $\omega = 2\pi f$!

EM9 The first part is bookwork. In part (b), note that, if the system is frictionless, energy considerations require the back e.m.f. at maximum speed to be equal and opposite to the driving e.m.f.

EM10 In the first part of the problem, apply the laws of electromagnetic induction to show that, when the ring is falling with velocity v, the flux cut per second is $2\pi r B v$ and hence the current in the ring is ABv/ρ_{Al}, where A is the cross-sectional area of the metal and ρ_{Al} its resistivity.

The final constant velocity is reached when the downward gravitational force is balanced by the upward electromagnetic force, $BIl \ (= BI2\pi r)$.

EM11 Note that a potential difference must be measured between *two* points. Many students become confused by talking about the p.d. at a point. Follow the advice in the question and think of the p.d. between the centre of the wheel and different points on the rim. This p.d. will be different depending on the point chosen on the rim because two e.m.f.'s are generated due to cutting lines of flux. One arises from the rotation of the wheel and is the same between the centre and all points on the rim. The other arises from the linear motion of the wheel and is not the same for all points on the rim.

If the rim makes n revolutions per second, $v = 2\pi r n$. The area swept out each second due to rotation is $\pi r^2 n = rv/2$. Hence the e.m.f. between the hub and rim is $rBv/2$ radially outwards.

Use the same idea to find the e.m.f. due to linear motion.

EM12 First consider the action of the rotating disc in a constant magnetic field.

It is easiest to think of a single spoke, of length a, making contact within a fixed rim, as shown in Fig. EM12.1. Contact is made to the axle of the spoke and to the rim. A constant, uniform magnetic field of flux density B is applied normal to the plane of the rim.

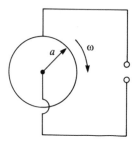

Fig. EM12.1

As the spoke rotates with uniform angular velocity ω, the area it sweeps out in time δt is $a^2\omega\,\delta t/2$. The number of lines of magnetic flux cut is $\delta\Phi = Ba^2\omega\delta t/2$. The rate of change of flux linkage is thus $\delta\Phi/\delta t = Ba^2\omega/2$. If the spoke makes n revolutions in unit time, then $n = \omega/2\pi$ and $\delta\Phi/\delta t = n\pi a^2 B$.

The magnitude of the e.m.f. induced between the contacts to the axle and the rim is thus $n\pi a^2 B$.

It is fairly easy to see that a uniform conducting disc, with contacts applied between the axle and a single point on the rim, is equivalent to the rotating spoke of Fig. EM12.1.

The field inside the solenoid has flux density equal to $\mu_0 NI$. If I were constant, the rotating disc would generate a constant induced e.m.f. of $n\pi a^2\,N\mu_0 I$. In this example, the current I varies sinusoidally, so an alternating e.m.f. is displayed on the oscilloscope.

The case of the stationary disc may be more puzzling. You may be tempted to think that, because the magnetic field is changing periodically, there ought to be an alternating induced e.m.f. between the axle and rim. However, the radius vector between axle and rim does not link any flux, so the induced e.m.f. is zero.

This example is based on a classic experiment to determine the value of the ohm absolutely.

EM13 The first part is bookwork. For the second part, note that (1) a capacitor and inductor in parallel are equivalent to a capacitor and inductor in closed circuit as in the circuit given in the question, (2) the final voltage on C_1 corresponds to transfer of all the energy from one capacitor to the other.

If you now consider carefully the energy changes that occur when a fixed charge oscillates between a capacitor and inductor connected in this way, the correct switching sequence should become apparent.

EM14 (a) Since the coil has no resistance, the back e.m.f. $L\,dI/dt$ equals the applied voltage. The required equation follows from a simple integration.

(b) Recall that, in an $L-R$ series circuit, the current decays exponentially with time constant L/R. Hence, the graph should be linear up to 0.5 s, followed by rapid exponential decay. Note that the final current is not zero because the solenoid is connected to a d.c. supply.

EM15 From the standard expression for the flux density in the solenoid, calculate the flux through each turn and hence the total flux linkage. This is equal to the product of the self-inductance and the current.

Energy has the same dimensions $(\mathrm{M\,L^2T^{-2}})$ or base units $(\mathrm{kg\,m^2\,s^{-2}})$ whether it is magnetic or any other sort of energy. The dimensions or base units of self-inductance can easily be obtained from the defining equation $E = -L\,dI/dt$. The total magnetic energy in the solenoid is obtained by combining the expressions for B, U and L. This is then divided by the volume of the solenoid.

The resistance R of the wire in the solenoid is $2\pi rnl\rho/A$. The time for the current in an $L-R$ circuit to fall to $1/e$ of its initial value (the time constant) is L/R; this is also the time for the flux density to decay to $1/e$ of the initial value. To obtain the time, merely divide the expression for L by that for R.

EM16 Equating gravitational and electromagnetic torques leads to

$$I = mg/2Bl$$

and

$$I = \frac{1}{R}\frac{d\phi}{dt}$$

at all times. At the instant when the angle between AD or BC and the horizontal is θ,

$$\Phi = BA\sin\theta,$$

thus

$$I = \frac{AB}{R}\frac{d(\sin\theta)}{dt} = \frac{AB}{R}\cos\theta\frac{d\theta}{dt}.$$

Hence the time taken for the wire to turn through a further small angle $\delta\theta$ is given by

$$\delta t = \frac{2l(AB)^2}{Rmg} \cos \theta \, \delta\theta.$$

Integrate to find the total time from $\theta = 0$ rad to $\pi/2$ rad.

EM17 When the disc rotates, an e.m.f. is generated. This causes a current to flow through the solenoid and this will cause an additional magnetic field. Note that this extra field can act either with or against the Earth's field, depending on the direction of the current. Erroneous application of Lenz' law might lead you to think that the current had to cause a field that would oppose B_0. This is not so. This induced current acts in such a way that its effect opposes the motion of the disc, not the Earth's magnetic field. Let the flux density due to the current in the solenoid be B. Then the total flux density

$$B' = B_0 \pm B.$$

Now

$$I = \frac{\omega}{2\pi} \frac{AB'}{R},$$

where ω is the angular velocity, A the area and R the resistance of the disc, and $B = \mu_0 nI$. These equations lead to

$$B' = B_0 \bigg/ \left(1 \pm \frac{\mu_0 nA\omega}{2\pi R}\right).$$

Hence solve for I. Draw graphs showing how I varies with ω for both directions of rotation. Note that B', and hence I, tend to infinity when the coil rotates such that B is in the *same* direction as B_0 and

$$1 - \frac{\mu_0 nA\omega}{2\pi R} = 0 \qquad \text{or} \qquad \omega = \frac{2\pi R}{\mu_0 nA}.$$

Satisfy yourself that this would not happen in practice.

EM18 Make the approximation that the force between two circular turns of the spring is the same as that between two straight wires, each of the same length as one turn of the coil, and separated by the same distance. When there is a current I in the coil, there will be an *attractive* force ΔF between the turns given by $2\pi\mu_0 I^2/2\pi(d + x)$, in the opposite direction to the force of extension produced by the load. By Hooke's law, the extension is proportional to the load, or $\Delta x/x = \Delta F/F$. Combine these expressions to calculate the fractional change $\Delta x/x$.

EM19   The first two parts are bookwork. For part (c), recall that the field energy associated with an inductor is $LI^2/2$; and, for part (d), that the work done by a battery to create extra flux $\delta\Phi$ is $I\delta\Phi$.

For the final part, you will have to think quite carefully about all the energy changes in the system. Try to satisfy yourself that if the spring is extended and then the current of 10 A passes: (i) the battery will supply energy as the inductance of the coil decreases (i.e. the coil shortens); (ii) part of this extra energy from the battery will appear as extra field energy; (iii) part will be converted to mechanical work to lift the 2.0 g mass.

EM20   The instantaneous value of the magnetic flux density near the centre of the solenoid is $B = \mu_0 nI/L$, where n is the total number of turns and L the length of the solenoid (refer to question EM12 if necessary). Use this equation, the laws of electromagnetic induction and the ideas of the first part of the question to calculate the r.m.s. voltage induced in the small coil.

EM21   Since the current can be expressed in the form $I = I_0 \sin \omega t$, the formula $F = BIl$ may be used to find an equation for the force on the coil in terms of $\sin \omega t$. Now $F = ma$ leads to an equation of the form

$$\ddot{x} = A \sin \omega t,$$

where x is the displacement of the coil. It is reasonable to assume that, in the steady state, the movement of the coil will be sinusoidal, following the stimulus provided by the current.

Hence let

$$x = x_0 \sin \omega t$$

and

$$\ddot{x} = -x_0 \omega^2 \sin \omega t.$$

Comparison of the two equations for $\ddot{x}$ shows that

$$x_0 = -A/\omega^2.$$

(Has the minus sign any physical significance?)

Alternatively, two integrations of $\ddot{x} = A \sin \omega t$ yield the same result, provided the velocity of the coil $\dot{x}$ is set equal to zero when $\cos \omega t = 0$ and the displacement of the coil x is set equal to zero when $\sin \omega t = 0$.

These conditions also assume the steady state, with the initial transient responses no longer significant.

EM22   The basic transformer equation and Ohm's law are all that are required here.

EM23 Recall that maximum power is transferred into the load when the resistance of the load is equal to the resistance of the circuit (generator plus transformer in this case) supplying power to it. The effective resistance of generator plus transformer as 'seen' by the load can be found by noting that the power actually delivered by the generator at current I_p will be the same as that appearing across the load at current I_s.

In a transformer, the energy is stored temporarily in the magnetic field associated with the coils. With an iron-cored transformer, there is a large back e.m.f. and this means that the stored magnetic field energy increases only slowly. At high frequencies, the polarity of the supply reverses before this magnetic field has been fully established and hence the power that can be drawn by the secondary circuit is greatly reduced.

EM24 The electron beam enters the region of magnetic field along a radius of the cylindrical volume. The velocity v of the electrons is thus at right angles to the flux density B. The electrons experience a force perpendicular to both v and B, and move along the arc of a circle of radius R, as indicated in Fig. EM24.1.

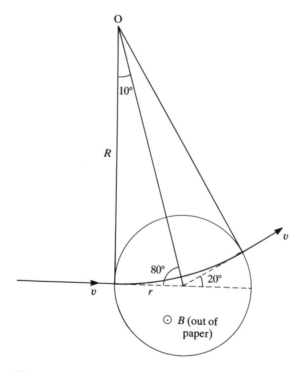

Fig. EM24.1

They emerge from the cylindrical volume along a radius, having experienced a total deflection of 20°. Simple trigonometry shows that $r/R = \tan 10°$.

The condition for circular motion in the magnetic field is

$$Bev = m_e v^2 / R,$$

so that

$$v = reB/(m_e \tan 10°).$$

Substitution of the values in the question leads to the result $v = 5.1 \times 10^7 \, \text{m s}^{-1}$. This solution neglects relativistic effects.

M25 This problem requires the standard equations that apply to an electron moving in electrostatic and magnetic fields. Remember that the magnetic field can only affect the velocity component that is at right angles to the field.

The magnetic flux density B and the magnetic field intensity H are related by $B = \mu_0 H$. The constant K is $8\pi^2/\mu_0^2$.

M26 Consider the time spent by the electron between the deflector plates. The electron emerges undeflected if the impulses to either side of the axis are equal and opposite. For a single electron, this would occur in the situation shown in Fig. EM26.1 if the electron entered at time t_A but not if it entered at time t_B. For the impulses to cancel for *all* electrons that enter this region at different times, the period of the deflecting a.c. potential must equal the transit time for an electron through the plate system. Then each electron is exposed to a full cycle of deflections.

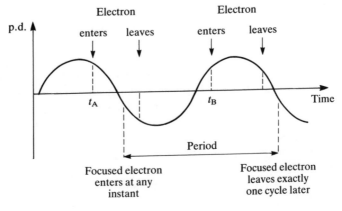

Fig. EM26.1

Show that, in general, electrons are focused if

$$\frac{e}{m_e} = \frac{f^2 x^2}{2n^2 V}$$

where n is an integer.

EM27 (a) The product mass × acceleration of the proton will be equal to the electrical force on it. By writing this product as $mv\, dv/dx$ and integrating twice, the value of t may be found in terms of the distance between the plates, assumed along the x-direction.

(b) There is no force due to the magnetic field initially because the proton has zero velocity. Subsequently, if the magnetic field is small, the deflection in the magnetic field will also be small and it may be assumed to a first approximation that the proton is always travelling in a direction normal to the plates.

The velocity of the proton due to the electric field is first found at any time t. The magnetic field will then cause the proton to accelerate along the y axis. Try to show that

$$m\ddot{y} = Be(eE/m)t.$$

This equation may be integrated twice to give y. The initial conditions $y = 0$, $\dot{y} = 0$ at $t = 0$ must be used to eliminate two constants of integration.

Since the force on the proton due to the magnetic field always acts normal to both B and v, if B is large enough to alter the direction of motion appreciably, the direction of the magnetic force will no longer act along the y-axis.

EM28 If the ions are travelling along the z-axis and both E and B are acting along the x-axis, they will produce deflections in the x- and y-directions, respectively.

If it is also assumed that the deflections of an ion while travelling between the plates are small, the important quantities are the velocities v_x and v_y with which the ions leave the plates; this is so because the ions will continue to travel in straight lines at constant speeds once there are no forces acting on them. You may find it helpful to use x and y to decribe what happens while an ion is travelling between the plates and X and Y for the final displacements on the screen.

Use the normal force equations to show that $v_x = EeL/mv_z$, where v_z is the speed at which ions are travelling along the z-axis and $v_y = BeL/m$. When writing down expressions for X and Y, introduce the time of travel from the moment an ion leaves the plates until it reaches the screen t. Then substitute $t = D/v_z$ and finally eliminate v_z.

When estimating E and B, if the positive ions are assumed to be protons, the only difficult part is choosing a value for v_z. Suggest a reason why $10^6\,\mathrm{m\,s^{-1}}$ might be a reasonable choice.

M29 This interesting problem in projectile motion is based on the fact that a charged particle moving with velocity v in a region where a uniform magnetic field of flux density B acts normal to v experiences a force equal to Bqv, where q is the charge on the particle, at right angles to both v and B.

Figure EM29.2 shows the relative directions of the electron velocity v and the flux density B as the electron enters the magnetic field.

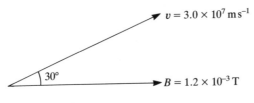

$v = 3.0 \times 10^7\,\mathrm{m\,s^{-1}}$

$30°$

$B = 1.2 \times 10^{-3}\,\mathrm{T}$

Fig. EM29.2

Resolve v into the components $v\cos 30°$ along the direction of the field and $v\sin 30°$ perpendicular to the field. Because the $v\cos 30°$ component is in the same direction as the magnetic field, there is no magnetic force on this component of the electron's motion, and the electron continues to move in the direction of the field with this velocity. Considering the component of velocity at right angles to the field, the electron will experience a force at right angles to both $v\sin 30°$ and to the field, causing circular motion in a plane perpendicular to the field. The combination of uniform motion along the direction of the field and circular motion perpendicular to it is a helix.

The condition for circular motion is that the magnetic force on the electron provides the centripetal force. Thus

$$Bev\sin\theta = m_e(v\sin\theta)^2/r.$$

(Note that $v\sin\theta$ appears on both sides of the equation, not v on one side and $v\sin\theta$ on the other.) Substitute in this equation and solve for r. The time t for one revolution is given by the circumference of the circle divided by the appropriate velocity component $v\sin\theta$. The pitch p is the distance travelled along the field direction in the time for one revolution and is obtained from $(v\cos\theta)t$.

The frequency of the electromagnetic radiation associated with the acceleration of this electron is equal to the frequency of the helical motion, which is simply $1/t$. The wavelength is obtained from $\lambda = c/f$.

EM30   (a) In deriving the expression for the Hall voltage and in subsequent calculations, it is very easy to become confused with directions and signs. First set up a reference system of coordinate axes, as shown in Fig. EM30.2.

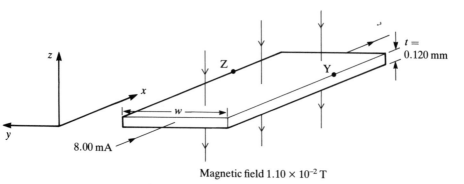

Fig. EM30.2

Let w be the width of the sample and t its thickness; let it contain number density n of charge carriers, each with charge se (where s is the sign, $+$ or $-$, and $e = 1.6 \times 10^{-19}$ C).

The conventional current I is flowing in the $+x$ direction: if the charge carriers are positive, they too flow in the $+x$ direction but, if they are negative, they are going in the $-x$ direction. To be general, we can say that carriers of charge se will move in the sx direction.

The principle of the Hall effect is that, in equilibrium, the magnetic and electric forces on the carriers cancel. The magnetic force on the carriers is Bev in the $+y$ direction. If the electric force is to balance this, $E = -Bv$ in the $+y$ direction. Hence $V_{ZY} = sBvw$, where v is the drift speed of the carriers. But v is also given by $v = I/ntwe$, so that $V_{ZY} = sBI/nte$.

In this example, we see that V_{ZY} is positive, so $s = +$ and the charge carriers are positive holes. Since $n = BI/V_{ZY}te$, substitution of the values in the question leads to $n = 4.0 \times 10^{19}$ m^{-3}.

(b) In metals, n is of the order of 10^{29} m^{-3}, so even if t were 0.01 mm (which is very thin) and I were 1 A (very large for such a thin conductor) and $B = 1$ T (also very large), V would be only about 6 μV. Thus, under any reasonable measuring conditions, it is not possible to get a usefully large signal from a metal Hall probe.

Atomic and nuclear physics

A1 In the second part, you will have to assume that all or virtually all the electrical energy is converted into heat. This is quite a good approximation here since only about 1% of the electron energy is converted into X-ray energy. However, this is only true for low-energy X-ray sets. In a linear accelerator working, say, at 16 MeV, a much higher proportion of the energy is converted into X-rays.

A2 This is a simple exercise in quantitative deductions from an energy level diagram.

In (a), you must first appreciate that the energy required to remove an electron from the K-level is given by the difference between the energy of an electron in the K-level and an electron at infinity, i.e. 3.00×10^{-15} J.

In (b), the energy released when an L-electron loses energy by moving to a vacancy in the K-level is given by the difference in energies of these levels. Use the relation $\Delta E = hf = hc/\lambda$ to find the wavelength of the X-ray photon in part (c).

If, on the other hand, the energy ΔE is used to cause the emission of an Auger electron, as in part (d), note that some of the energy is used in raising the potential energy of the M-electron from -3×10^{-17} J to zero, and the remainder appears as kinetic energy.

Determination of the kinetic energies of Auger electrons allows the identification of atoms from which these electrons have been emitted, in just the same way as wavelength measurements on optical or X-ray spectra lead to the identification of the atoms from which these photons have been emitted.

A3 It is immediately obvious that any body in orbit around a more massive body has kinetic energy $mv^2/2$. It is not so obvious that, relative to zero at infinity, the body also has potential energy. If the bodies are small but charged, most of the potential energy is electrostatic. Show that the potential energy when the orbital radius is r is $-e^2/4\pi\varepsilon_0 r$. [What is the analogous expression for gravitational potential energy? See question M.5. How may this expression be used to justify that gravitational effects may be neglected in the presence of electrostatic effects?] The minus sign signifies a loss of potential energy relative to zero at infinity.

Now use the inverse square law of force, $F \propto e^2/r^2$, and $F = mv^2/r$ to find the total energy, kinetic plus potential.

Check that ignoring the potential energy gives the right answer with the wrong sign. [Would this still be true if the force of attraction varied as $1/r^3$?]

Ignoring the potential energy results in an apparent paradox if one considers the effect on the energy of the body of a small decrease in the radius r. For equilibrium, $v^2 \propto 1/r$ from above, so if r decreases the body must travel faster. Therefore, the kinetic energy will *increase*. But since the force is attractive, work is done by the moving body when it approaches the massive body so its total energy must *decrease*. This is found to be true if due allowance is also made for the change in potential energy.

You will save a lot of repetition if you use a *general* expression $nh/2\pi$ (where n is an integer) for the angular momentum and substitute appropriate values of n at the end of the calculation. The general expression for E will be

$$E = \frac{me^4}{8\varepsilon_0^2 h^2} \frac{1}{n^2},$$

and changes in E are proportional to $(1/n_1^2 - 1/n_2^2)$.

A4 This question provides a useful introduction to the ideas of wave mechanics. The electron has a wavelength associated with it and this may be derived from the de Broglie relationship, $p = h/\lambda$. Only modes of wave motion that produce a standing wave pattern are allowed, and this leads to quantisation of the energy levels. Do not confuse these electron waves with photon waves. The energy of the electrons is given by $E = p^2/2m$ and not by $E = hc/\lambda$.

A5 (a) The first part follows directly by combining the de Broglie relationship $\lambda = h/p$, the standing wave condition that the orbit must be an integral number of wavelengths and an expression for the angular momentum of the electron (mvr).

(b) Write down values for the total energy and the total angular momentum of the system; then note that the latter must also equal $nh/2\pi$, where n is an integer.

(c) The lowest energy level is a standing wave with λ equal to twice the length of the box. Write down a general expression for λ in terms of the length of the box and n, an integer that is determined by the standing wave pattern in the box. Hence find the momentum p and recall that $E = p^2/2m$ is a useful expression for kinetic energy.

When these ideas are applied to the speck of dust, $n = 3 \times 10^{15}$: thus, n cannot be distinguished from $n + 1$ and the concept of energy quantisation is meaningless.

A6 (a) The number of hydrogen atoms in 2 g (care, not in 2 kg!) of the liquid is $2 \times 6.0 \times 10^{23}$, the volume being $2/(90 \times 10^3)\,\text{m}^3$.

Hence, if each atom is assumed to be a sphere of radius a, the value of a may be calculated.

(b) (i) The product of mass $\times$ acceleration of the electron in its circular orbit must be equal to the electrostatic force of attraction between the electron and proton; hence ω may be calculated.

(ii) The *total* energy of the electron (kinetic and potential) may be written down as the sum of two terms and the value for ω^2 derived in the previous part of the question may be used to simplify the expression to a single term. See the advice for question A3.

(c) You must make sure you can show that the total energy of the electron is $-e^2/8\pi\varepsilon_0 a$ before attempting this part. Now assume the electron has reached an arbitrary distance r from the nucleus. Its energy is $-e^2/8\pi\varepsilon_0 r$ and the rate of change of energy with time, dE/dt, may be found in terms of dr/dt.

This equation has two variables r and ω, but ω may be found in terms of r (and the corresponding original, constant values ω_0 and a) by conservation of angular momentum.

This leads to an equation in which the only variables are r and t and an integral of the form $\int kx^4 dx$ now gives t.

A7 This is a fairly straightforward question provided you think about the *symmetry* of the problem. Try to apply the law of conservation of momentum in your head rather than writing down equations with a lot of unknowns that must be eliminated by laborious algebra. You should go on to show that the energy comes from conversion of a mass of about $1.7 \times 10^{-32}\,\text{kg}$.

A8 Consider the motion carefully and satisfy yourself that, at the position of closest approach, each α-particle will be travelling with the same velocity v. Use conservation of momentum to find v. Now work out the loss of kinetic energy of the α-particle from the start of the motion to this position of closest approach. This will be equal to the gain in electrostatic potential energy $\int_{\infty}^{x_0}(-F)\,dx$, where x_0 is the closest distance of approach.

An alternative method is to look at the motion in a reference frame where the centre of mass remains at rest. If the initial α-particle velocity is v_0, show that, to an observer moving in the same direction at velocity $v_0/2$, the centre of mass remains at rest and the particles approach each other with equal velocities. [You may like to show that, in a simple collision process, the laws of conservation of momentum and energy both still apply if an arbitrary velocity u is added to the velocity of each particle. This is quite general and applies to unequal masses but the equations are simpler if you assume equal masses.]

In this moving frame of reference, the closest approach will be when the α-particles come to rest. As before, the kinetic energy will be stored as electrostatic potential energy, and in either method an integral of the form $\int kx^{-2}\,dx$ is involved.

A9 The first part should cause no problem if you are careful in applying the laws of conservation of momentum and energy.

The second part can be solved similarly by assigning momentum hf/c and energy hf to the photon. Since the photon has very little momentum, its direction of motion will be reversed by the collision and you will need to simplify your equations (see the guidance for question M21) by using the fact that the velocities of the heavy particles are much less than the speed of light.

Note that the results of this experiment made a valuable contribution to the discovery of the neutron.

A10 A careful drawing (see Fig. A10.1) and the instructions in the question should suffice for the first two parts. Recall that an expression for angular momentum about a fixed point distance r away is mvr.

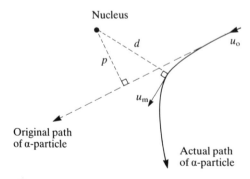

Fig. A10.1

For the final part, consider unit area of foil. The total number of nuclei is Nx and α-particles pass within a distance d of a gold nucleus if their initial path passes within a distance p of that nucleus. Hence the fraction is $Nx\pi p^2$ and the rest follows.

A11 When light is incident on a photo-emissive metal surface, there is a certain maximum wavelength above which (minimum quantum energy below which) no electrons are released. This is because the electrons generated must first overcome the work function of the metal, i.e. the potential barrier at the surface of the metal. If the sphere becomes negatively charged, this is equivalent to changing its work function.

A12 Use the Einstein photoelectric emission equation to obtain the maximum kinetic energy of the emitted electrons in terms of the wavelength of the incident light and the work function of the metal, and hence find v_m.

The remaining parts of the question are an example of projectile motion. The electric field between the plates gives the electron an acceleration a normal to the screen; its initial component of velocity normal to the screen is zero. The time t taken to travel the distance y is thus given by $y = at^2/2$.

Because the electron has a constant component of velocity v_m parallel to the plate, its trajectory is a parabola, as shown in Fig. A12.3.

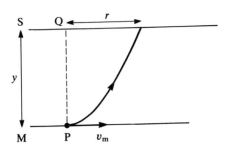

Fig. A12.3

It will strike the screen a distance r away from the point Q directly opposite its origin on the plate M. Electrons similar to E will be emitted from P in all directions along the surface of M, and each will follow a parabolic path to S, striking S at a distance r from Q. This will lead to a bright circular disc on the screen. Because the transverse velocity v_m is unaffected by the field, r is given by $v_m t$.

From the previous part, you will have found that r is proportional to $V^{-1/2}$. Increasing the potential increases the acceleration of the electron, so that the transit time and the radius of the disc are reduced. Increasing the potential by a factor of 4 reduces the radius by a factor of 2.

A13 In this question, you apply familiar principles to what will probably be an unfamiliar situation. The approach here is only approximate; the full theory requires relativistic equations. Nevertheless, the approximate method leads to the correct relations.

(a) Because momentum is conserved, the vector representing the momentum of the incident X-ray photon must be equal to the vector sum of the momentum of the scattered X-ray photon and the momentum of the recoil electron. Display this condition in the closed triangle of the vector diagram.

(b) You will need the cosine rule $a^2 = b^2 + c^2 - 2bc \cos A$ to solve the vector triangle. Applying this formula,

$$(m_e v)^2 = (hf/c)^2 + [h(f - \Delta f)/c]^2 - 2h^2 f(f - \Delta f)(\cos \theta)/c^2.$$

Expand the second squared term on the right-hand side and neglect terms in $(\Delta f)^2$.

(c) The energy before the interaction is the photon energy hf. This must be equal to the energy of the scattered photon plus the kinetic energy of the recoil electron.

(d) Since $c = f\lambda$, $\Delta f/f = -\Delta\lambda/\lambda$ and $c = (f - \Delta f)(\lambda + \Delta\lambda)$. Combine the momentum and energy equations from (b) and (c) and convert f and Δf to λ and $\Delta\lambda$.

(e) The graph has the shape of a $(1 - \cos\theta)$ curve, with a maximum at $\cos\theta = -1$, i.e. $\theta = 180°$, where the maximum wavelength shift is $2h/m_e c$. The condition $\theta = 180°$ is equivalent to a head-on collision between the X-ray photon and the stationary electron, a situation that would be expected to lead to the maximum loss of photon energy and hence the maximum wavelength shift.

A14 Although this physical idea may be new to you, the actual calculation requires straightforward application of the equation that expresses the equivalence of mass and energy.

A15 If the particle-like properties of the γ-ray are considered, then this problem is similar to the collision of more massive bodies. Conservation of energy and momentum apply and both these quantities can be calculated for the γ-ray. Remember that some of the γ-ray energy (most of it in fact) will reappear as the masses of the β-particles according to Einstein's mass–energy equation. Only the residual energy will be available to give the β-particles kinetic energy.

A full answer to the last part really requires careful consideration of the type of collision that will result in transfer of maximum momentum to the β-particles. Try to show that it is about 8×10^{-23} N s in this question.

One final piece of advice for this and similar problems: at this level of physics, answers for velocities that exceed the speed of light are almost certainly wrong and at least deserve comment even if you cannot find your error!

A16 Remember that conservation of momentum as well as conservation of energy will apply.

A17 This is one of the few problems where it is no real help to work in algebraic symbols. Divide the calculation into three parts and work out each answer separately.

(a) Find out how many carbon-14 atoms were present in 10 g of carbon when the wood died.

(b) Use the differential form of the radioactive decay law to find out how many carbon-14 atoms there are now.

(c) Use the radioactive decay law again to relate answers (a) and (b) and so find the answer.

Remember to convert $t_{1/2}$, the half-life, to λ, the characteristic decay constant.

A18 Consider the first scheme:

$$^{238}_{92}\text{U} \rightarrow {}^{206}_{82}\text{Pb} + 10\text{p} + 22\text{n}.$$

The binding energy of the Pb atom is less than that of the U atom, by 188 MeV. Therefore, the reaction is only possible if the other products have a binding energy that exceeds this difference. Since protons and neutrons have no binding energy (being primary particles), the reaction is not energetically possible.

In the second scheme,

$$^{238}_{92}\text{U} \rightarrow {}^{206}_{82}\text{Pb} + 8^4_2\text{He} + 6\text{e}^-,$$

the α-particles have binding energy, so the reaction may be possible. The total binding energy on the left-hand side is 1801 MeV. On the right-hand side, the total binding energy of the lead and of eight α-particles is 1839.4 MeV. The six electrons are of nuclear origin, and their energy of formation ($6m_e c^2$) must be subtracted, giving a net binding energy of 1836.2 MeV. Since the net binding energy on the right-hand side of the scheme exceeds that on the left-hand side, this scheme is possible. Approximately 35 MeV of energy is available as energy of the α-particles, β-particles and some γ-rays.

Apply the radioactive decay equation to the two uranium isotopes.

For $^{238}_{92}U$, $N_1 = N_0 \exp(-\alpha t)$, where $\alpha = \ln 2/(4.5 \times 10^9)$ year^{-1}; for $^{235}_{92}U$, $N_2 = N_0 \exp(-\beta t)$, where $\beta = \ln 2/(7.13 \times 10^8)$ year^{-1}. Take the ratio of N_1 to N_2:

$$N_1/N_2 = \exp[(\beta - \alpha)t].$$

Take logarithms of both sides:

$$\ln(N_1/N_2) = (\beta - \alpha)t = (\ln 2)t[1/(7.13 \times 10^8) - 1/(4.5 \times 10^9)].$$

i.e.

$$(\ln 137.8)/(\ln 2) = t[1/(7.13 \times 10^8) - 1/(4.5 \times 10^9)].$$

Solving this equation leads to $t = 6 \times 10^9$ years.

A19   Since the total number of atoms at any time is constant, $N_s = N_0 - N_t$, where N_0 is the number of radioactive atoms at time $t = 0$. The given equation follows directly.

Your graphs should be as shown in Fig. A19.1.

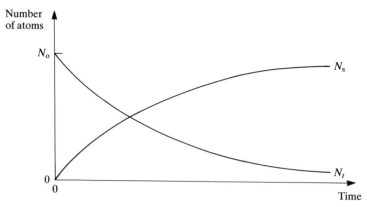

Fig. A19.1

To determine the numbers of α-particles and β^--particles, note that only α-emission changes the nucleon (mass) number (by 4 for each α-particle emitted). Having determined the number of α-particles, the number of β^--particles may be found by balancing the charge.

To estimate the age of the rock, write down equations relating N_{207} to N_{235} and N_{206} to N_{238}. Divide one by the other and recall that $\lambda T_{1/2} = \ln 2$. For further advice see question A18.

It would be difficult to solve for t but substitution of $t = 10^9$ years should show that the LHS and RHS of the equation agree to about 3%.

Various assumptions are made. Perhaps the most important is that there was no ^{206}Pb or ^{207}Pb in the rock sample originally.

A20 The number of radioactive atoms N will continue to increase until their rate of production (i.e., R, given) is exactly balanced by their rate of decay. You should be able to show that $R = \lambda N_{max}$, where λ is the decay constant.

For the second part, the more general case must be considered. Show that the increase in the number of radioactive atoms in a small time interval is given by the differential equation

$$dN = (R - \lambda N)\,dt.$$

This is a relatively easy equation to solve if the suggested substitutions are made.

A21 This problem is fairly straightforward, even though the situation may be unfamiliar.

After converting the half-life to a decay constant, the radioactive exponential decay law may be used to correct for decay over a 30 day period (a factor of 1.58). A dilution factor must then be applied to allow for the fact that only a sample of oil has been measured; remember also to convert minutes into seconds.

A22 First calculate the rate of rise in temperature of the liquid (about $1.25 \times 10^{-4}\,\mathrm{K\,s^{-1}}$). The remainder of the first part is straightforward.

In the second part, find the number of beta-particles required to generate $10\,\mathrm{mW}$ and substitute in the normal radioactive decay equation.